Mrs. Boulé -

Thanks for all your help in C.C.D. and . . .

God bless

Howard Rowe

Brothers of the Faith

STEPHEN C. NEILL

Brothers of the Faith

ABINGDON PRESS

NEW YORK NASHVILLE

BROTHERS OF THE FAITH

Library of Congress Catalog Card Number: 60-9201

SET UP, PRINTED, AND BOUND BY THE PARTHENON PRESS, AT NASHVILLE, TENNESSEE, UNITED STATES OF AMERICA

PREFACE

For three almost literally killing years I was engaged on the preparation of the *History of the Ecumenical Movement, 1517-1948*. That was not an official work in the sense of representing a special World Council of Churches view of history—the World Council as such has no view of history other than a concern that it should be accurately and impartially recorded. Nevertheless, a work sponsored by so many august bodies inevitably took on something of an official aura; the personal factor had to be a good deal played down, and many things that we would have liked to include had to be excluded for a variety of personal reasons.

This, by contrast, is an entirely personal work. In 1924 I attended the Birmingham Conference on Christian Politics, Economics and Citizenship (COPEC). This means that for more than thirty-five years I have lived ecumenically. In large sections of this book I am writing about events that I have lived through; many of the leading participants to whom I refer by name are my friends. I have tried to record things as I have seen and experienced them. This means that any other writer would have recorded them from a slightly different angle. But this is the way in which history ultimately emerges—never with perfect accuracy—from the recollections of many men checked against the documents and records of the time. Everything that I have here stated has been checked against contemporary documents, from which fairly long citations have been given. I hope that in this way what is primarily a personal record may be found also to have a certain objective quality.

There are shadows in the picture as well as lights. There always are in any true picture of the Church, and always will be, as long as we walk by faith and not by sight. The path of ecumenical endeavour is always an uphill road. Many things aimed at have not been attained; many apparently fruitful efforts have ended in frustration. There are many corners in the road. Time and again the summit has seemed to be in view, but when that point has been reached, it has merely opened out the view of another and more distant summit. Yet for all the disappointments and frustrations those of us who have lived ecumenically through these years have felt that what we were engaged on was worth while.

STEPHEN C. NEILL

CONTENTS

Introduction

The Ecumenical Era Arrives

THE ECUMENICAL MOVEMENT EXISTS TO WORK FOR TWO GREAT aims—the unity and the renewal of the church.

It has sometimes been thought that these two aims are coincident—that, if we can unite separated churches, there will immediately be a release of spiritual power, and that, if a renewal of the life of the churches takes place, closer fellowship will naturally result. History shows us that this assumption is not justified by the facts. We can now study a great many processes of church union and the history of the united churches that have sprung from them. In every case the union has produced many advantages; it just is not the case that renewal of spiritual life has always been included among those advantages. And sometimes spiritual renewal has resulted in fresh divisions. So it was in England in the eighteenth century, when the Methodist movement breathed on the stagnant waters of English Christianity. Had things been other than they were, that great movement might have been kept within the Church of England. As it turned out, renewal was responsible for yet another division in the Christian churches, a division that has not yet been completely healed.

Unity and renewal are both good things. Both must be eagerly sought, but it must not be too hastily assumed that one will follow in the train of the other.

As regards renewal, hardly anyone will be in disagreement. We none of us know a Christian church which is what it ought to be. The worship of the Christian churches is often uninteresting, the challenge they present anaemic, their witness tame, their attempts to grapple with social problems amateurish and less effective than those of others who do not profess and call themselves Christians. Individuals who claim the name of Christian are not always very different from their neighbors and sometimes seem less attractive than they; their lives are not always marked by overflowing joy and lovingkindness. These things are undeniable. Anything that tends to make things better than they are ought to have the uncompromising support of everyone.

As regards the unity of the churches it is unlikely that there will be such complete and immediate agreement.

Some will maintain frankly that Christian divisions are a good thing. It is only in this way that the full range of Christian truth has been worked out. A little rivalry between the churches is a good thing, it keeps them on their toes and prevents them from falling down into too easy a complacency and self-satisfaction.

Those who are not prepared to go as far as this may still feel that Christian divisions do not really matter very much and that no great effort need be expended on trying to reduce them. We have grown up accustomed to the sight of half a dozen churches in a single street. To decide which church you will belong to seems to be part of that freedom which the American citizen claims as his birthright. As a matter of fact an immense number of Americans do moreover from one church to another, in some cases several times in one lifetime, the change being motivated by residence, by dislike of a particular minister, by a preference for good music, or any one of twenty or thirty motives which really have nothing to do with the Christian faith or the responsibilities of Christian witness in the world. And why worry if different churches seem to meet the needs of different temperaments and different social levels in the population?

It must be admitted that things look rather different when we move from the familiar American scene to, let us say, South India. Here it is literally possible for two brothers, Hindus, to be sent to different schools and there to be converted to separate Christian churches which, now that they are Christians, will not allow them to receive the Holy Communion together. The Christ who, as we say, makes all men one has as a matter of fact introduced a deep and disastrous division. If you live on one side of a small stream and become a Christian, you will become a Danish Lutheran—that is the only Protestant church in your area. If you live on the other side of the stream and become a

Christian, you will join the American Dutch Reformed Church. At one time, in one square mile of Madras there were thirteen different churches. Which of them is the perplexed Hindu to join, if he wishes to follow Christ? The arguments in favor of having just one Christian church in such a region would seem to be strong.

We have to take seriously the situation in which we find ourselves. Today the Christian churches are threatened as they have not been threatened for a thousand years. In some lands they live under the perpetual menace of the communist colossus. In others secularism is eating away their very foundations. The ancient religions of the East are awakening, and in alliance with the new nationalism are sending out their missionaries to the West. In times of political danger party loyalties are forgotten; they give place to an intense sense of national loyalty and solidarity. It might seem only commonsense, if the Christian churches, realising their common peril, were to be driven to far closer fellowship and co-operation than exist among them today.

But these are all superficial reasons. Some Christians, reading the New Testament, seem to themselves to find a far deeper and more commanding reason for unity in the will of God himself. In Christ, we are told, there is neither Jew nor Greek, barbarian, Scythian, bond nor free, but all together have been made one new man in Jesus Christ. The first great problem of the early church was to make room in one and the same organization for Jew and Gentile, who in civil life had been kept so utterly separate from one another. The church, it seems, is meant to be the great international society in which at last all men will find a home. Already the church is the most international of societies. It exists on both sides of the iron curtain and of the bamboo curtain and of every other kind of curtain. It stretches far beyond the limits of the United Nations, for instance into Switzerland, resolutely neutral and therefore not a member of the United Nations Organization. Yet this great fact is robbed of its true significance by the endless divisions of Christians and by their failure ever to show to the world the inner unity that holds them together. Surely this is not what the New Testament means when it talks about the church as the body of Christ.

Now when we talk of a united church, it must not be supposed that we are thinking in terms of absolute uniformity. Even the Roman Catholic Church, which insists on greater uniformity than any other, permits the use of no less than twelve languages in the conduct of services; the idea that it insists on Latin everywhere is a common Protestant mistake. So if all the churches were at last able to come together, there ought to be room for a great variety of national expressions of the faith, of types and forms of worship, and so on. What it would mean, however, is that anyone who was a minister anywhere in the church would, by the same title, be a minister everywhere, and that anyone who was a communicant in any of the churches would be a communicant in them all. We are far from that today. In every international gathering of Christians our experience has always been the same—that it is impossible for them all to receive the Holy Communion together in the same service.

From the beginning of Christian history there have been divisions within the church; from the beginning there have been men and women consumed with a desire to see these divisions eliminated and unity restored. But this ecumenical desire and ecumenical service have taken different forms through the centuries.

In the early centuries the great instrument of unity was the Church Council. It was a great moment in the history of the church when for the first time, in A.D. 325, the Emperor Constantine ordered the bishops of the whole church to come together in the Council of Nicaea. Bishops are very human creatures; they have their weaknesses and their passions like anyone else. There is much that is sad, and some things that are discreditable in the history of these councils. Yet they did define the faith and exclude error. And through their records we can still feel breathing the earnest desire of these men of old time that the church of Christ should both be, and be seen to be, one in him.

The division that has affected us most deeply was that of the Reformation of the sixteenth century. In less than thirty years the divisions in Europe had hardened down, and the lines between Catholic and Protestant, as they were then drawn up, have hardly changed in four centuries. There is no country in the world in which this division is more sharply felt than in the United States.

Our history books tell us much about the divisions. They do not usually tell us much about the earnest attempts of good men to find a way back to unity. This was the age in which the ecumenical leaders were the theologians. Time and time again leaders on both sides met and really tried to understand one another and to see whether bridges could not be built from both sides. Perhaps they came nearer to agreement at Ratisbon in 1541 than ever before or since. But the differences were deep and comprehensive, and that is a division in the body of Christ which has so far resisted all attempts to heal it.

In the seventeenth century the work was taken up by dedicated individuals who gave their lives to the cause of unity. One of the most famous of these was the Scot, John Dury. His whole life was spent in endless travels from country to country trying to get churches and church leaders interested in one another and in the cause on which his heart was set. If not very much seemed to come from his efforts, that was not for lack of trying; perhaps the propitious moment for successful ecumenical effort had not yet come.

In the eighteenth century the rulers took a hand. Over almost the whole of Europe it was still taken for granted that the ruler had some responsibility in the sight of God for what his subjects believed as well as for what they did. The eighteenth century opens with some interesting negotiations between rulers in Britain and rulers in Germany (we must not forget that at that time the King of England was also Elector of Hanover); positive results were few, other than the translation of the English Prayer Book into German in 1704. Christian negotiations became too much mixed up in political affairs for any very useful results to be possible. Then, after the eighteenth century had merged into the nineteenth, the King of Prussia brought about the first great reunion in Christian history, with the formation of the Old Prussian Union in which his Lutheran and his Calvinist subjects were, after a fashion, brought together. Many did, and would now, regard this as a very unsatisfactory union, dependent far more on the will of the ruler than on any theological principle. But at least it deserves mention as the first of an increasing series.

The nineteenth century was the age of voluntary societies. Societies formed by good Christians for good purposes were numbered literally in hundreds. The important thing about many of them was that they cut right across the divisions of confession and denomination. One of the first of this type was the British and Foreign Bible Society, founded in 1804; from the start this had Anglicans and Free Churchmen on its committee. An even more famous example is the Young Men's Christian Association, the first of the great international Christian bodies and the great pioneer in developing national leadership in the lands of the younger churches. The basis of the Y.M.C.A. was personal faith in Jesus Christ and allegiance to him. The question of denominational affiliation hardly arose; it was taken for granted that the good member of a Y.M.C.A. would also be a loyal member of some church or other, but these enthusiastic young people found that their common loyalty to Jesus Christ bound them together, in spite of differences and divisions on many other levels.

The nineteenth century saw the development of Christian co-operation on a scale and in a variety of ways never imagined before. Not unnaturally this happened even more readily on "the mission field" than in the older countries. Traditions were less binding; the needs were more urgent. Christians were tiny groups isolated amid masses of unbelieving people. Almost inevitably they sought one another out and found that they could work together in countless ways. By the end of the century co-operation had become firmly established as a principle and perhaps had gone almost as far as it could go. Was a further step possible, and if so, what should that step be?

None of us can see far into the future. It is unlikely that any leading Christian, asked in the year 1900 to prophesy about the events that might be expected to take place in the Christian world in the succeeding sixty years, would have correctly predicted any of the things that are to be written in this book. The question that any reader of this brief summary of ecumenical activity through the centuries might well ask would be, "Where were the churches in all this?" The answer, strange but true, is that the churches as such took hardly any part at all in all this effort and on occasions opposed it. This was to be the great new beginning of the twentieth century.

Enter the churches. In this book we shall watch them enter very hesitantly, with many precautions and many backward glances, but impelled by a force that they could not resist. The twentieth century is the century of the churches. All the other forms of ecumenical activity still exist and have their part to play. But, increasingly as the years have passed, responsibility to work for the unity and renewal of the church has been seen to belong in the first place to the churches themselves and to no one else. How this has come to be recognized is really the subject of this book. This is the golden thread running through all the chapters and through all the multiplicity of subjects that has had to be discussed. The churches have entered on a new period of their history. Hesitantly and uncertainly they have been led to respond to a new call, a new vocation that has been laid on them in our time by the Head of the church himself.

I. Edinburgh 1910

John R. Mott and World Vision

AT EXACTLY 3 P.M., ON JUNE 14, 1910, THE PRESIDENT, LORD Balfour of Burleigh, rose to his feet. In half an hour the business had been done, and the first World Missionary Conference (to consider missionary problems in relation to the non-Christian world) had been constituted. The Conference had adopted the salutary rule that "the time allotted to each speaker in the discussion . . . shall not exceed seven minutes"—would that all other ecumenical gatherings had done the same! And it had accepted the resolution "that Mr. John R. Mott be appointed Chairman of the Conference in Committee, in accordance with Standing Order III."

Edinburgh 1910 was not by any means the first attempt to gather from all the world and from all the churches those interested in the missionary vocation of the church. 1960 marks the jubilee of Edinburgh 1910; it also marks the centenary of Liverpool 1860. In that year a conference had been held, attended by 126 members, of whom one was an Indian, the Rev. Behari Lal Singh. Other conferences had followed in 1878, 1888, and 1900 with increasing interest and participation. The Conference of 1900 called itself the "Ecumenical Conference," not because it claimed to represent all parts of the Christian church, but because it did represent missionary work in every region of the inhabited earth. But Edinburgh 1910 was different from all previous conferences in a number of highly significant ways.

In the first place there was a change in the purpose and the emphasis of the Conference. The aim of the previous meetings had been illumination, information, and inspiration. They had set themselves to draw together large numbers of people, to set before them reliable information as to the state of the church and its work in many parts of the world, and to stimulate them to greater devotion in Christian giving and service. "It was felt, however, that the time had now come for a more earnest study of the missionary enterprise, and that . . . the first aim should be to make the Conference as far as possible a consultative assembly." [1]

This decision did much to determine the character of the Conference and its membership. Careful steps had been taken to make the gathering really representative of the missionary work of the church, with the exception, of course, of the Roman Catholic Church, which was not represented. No less than 153 missionary bodies in various parts of the world sent delegates. Although the Conference was held in Britain, the British delegates were considerably outnumbered by those from America and the continent of Europe. But more important than this was the way in which those who organized the Conference had secured the co-operation and presence of a number of the ablest thinkers and statesmen in the whole Christian world. So here was Julius Richter of Germany, whose massive volumes are still our best authority for the early history of missions in various parts of the world, rubbing shoulders with a former Governor of Bombay. Charles Gore, the Anglo-Catholic Bishop of Birmingham, reckoned by many to have had at that time the most powerful mind in the Church of England, was there in company with famous leaders of the American churches such as Robert E. Speer. Nor must we forget the remarkable group of younger men who had been gathered together to serve as ushers. There was a notable scholar named William Temple, then twenty-seven years old, whose name will recur again and again in our pages. Another was John Baillie, later to be Principal of New College, Edinburgh, and at the time of writing one of the presidents of the World Council of Churches.

No conference had ever before been so carefully prepared for as this one. The main subject of the Conference had been divided up into eight themes and a commission appointed to deal with each of the eight. Questions were sent out to many hundreds of missionaries in the field; their answers had been carefully

[1] *World Missionary Conference: History, Records and Addresses,* p. 8. Edited by J. H. Oldham and used by permission of Harper and Brothers.

considered by the commissions and digested in their reports. So that whereas the previous conferences had started from zero, Edinburgh 1910 had before it, from the first moment, eight carefully prepared and weighty documents.

But in nothing was the Conference more remarkable than in its choice of a chairman.

John R. Mott, forty-five years old and at the very height of his powers, had never been a missionary, but he was called to preside over the greatest missionary gathering in history. A layman, he had the Archbishop of Canterbury and many other prelates sitting under his chairmanship. A life-long Methodist, he was recognized as the leader in a movement that has drawn together men and women from all the churches. An American to the tips of his fingers, he had made himself the very symbol of international fellowship and co-operation. Speaking hardly a word of any language but his own, he was to be the master of such polyglot assemblies as was this at Edinburgh.

Mott could be authoritarian, almost brutal in the Chair. He would give short shrift to any offender against the rules of procedure. Determined to get things done, he at times swept opposition out of his path and roused opposition by his dictatorial methods. But in a great international assembly he was at his best. Firm, courteous, conciliatory, he would see to it that every point of view was heard and that the due balance of order was observed in all the proceedings. The assembly had no reason to regret its choice; probably everyone present would have agreed with the judgment of the official history that "Dr. Mott presided . . . with promptitude and precision, with instinctive perception of the guidance required, and with a perfect union of firmness and Christian courtesy, of earnest purpose and timely humour, which won for him alike the deference and the gratitude of the members."[2]

But we must go back a little in our history to learn how all this had come about.

In the 1870's and 1880's a great renewal of interest in the Christian faith was sweeping through Britain and in particular was touching the ancient universities of Oxford and Cambridge.

[2] *Op. cit.*, p. 23.

In 1882 England was deeply stirred to learn that seven of the outstanding men at Cambridge—outstanding as athletes and in many other ways—were giving up everything to go out to China as missionaries under the China Inland Mission. As a result of this movement a group of Cambridge men crossed the Atlantic in order to carry their message to American universities. At Cornell J. E. K. Studd was drawn into contact with one young Methodist in particular. This young man had experienced a somewhat childish conversion at the age of thirteen, but now he was in a state of uncertainty regarding the Christian faith and regarding his own future course in life. Studd was used to bring him to a definite and uncompromising surrender to Jesus Christ. The young man's name was John Raleigh Mott.

If Mott did anything, he was likely to do it thoroughly. Once committed to Christ, it became the major task of his life to bring others to like commitment. For the first thing to be known about Mott is that all his life long he had the heart of an evangelist; what he wanted more than anything else was to proclaim to men and women the good news of new life in Jesus Christ.

One of the addresses he repeated a great many times was on "The Four Square Man." The phrase may have seemed to many of his hearers of those days to typify Mott himself. Massive in frame, simple, direct, advancing always as one who knew the direction in which he was going, he seemed often to have the force of a battleship moving effortlessly through the water. Mott could never speak in any terms other than those of the superlative. For him every hour was the decisive hour. Amused and kindly friends made collections of his favorite epithets, watched for their reappearance or for the appearance of a new one. "Every sentence is brought down like a blow; and, as when the heavy arm of some stone-breaker bangs blow on blow on the heart of a lump of stone, until it fairly smashes into fragments, not otherwise hammer the sentences of John R. Mott, with careful scientific deliberateness, until, at the end, the audience finds itself, in a word,—smashed." So said Temple Gairdner, himself no mean orator and chronicler of the great Conference. But as a wise and true interpreter he hastens to add, "Such consistent power is vested in no man save him in whom it daily accumulates by habitual communion with the one Source."[3]

Mott's work started in America, but he was very soon drawn outward into the international field. He was not, in the ordinary sense of the term, at all an imaginative man; yet he had a tremendous power of imaginative vision, and what he saw was the world. Few men can ever have had such capacity to hold the whole world for so long before their minds without losing control of the detail of the tasks that immediately lay to hand. One of his first great achievements in this field was the formation, in 1895 at Vadstena in Sweden, of the World's Student Christian Federation. This was not the first international Christian organization—it had been preceded by the World's Alliance of Young Men's Christian Associations and by the World's Young Women's Christian Association. But Mott was right in thinking that this new organization for students was destined to have special significance.

In the first place it was the instrument used to drive out thousands of the finest students of that and subsequent generations into missionary service in every part of the known world and to kindle in the minds of students who did not themselves feel the call to that special form of Christian service a sense of the worldwide Church, its mission, its task, and its struggles. Of those present at the Edinburgh Conference and of those who were to accept positions in the many movements which developed out of Edinburgh 1910, more than a few had come up through the Student Christian Movements and had received through them the vision of what it means to serve Christ in the modern age.

More than this, almost from the first Mott had seen what a tremendous power the W.S.C.F. could exercise in favor of the unity of the churches. Already in 1895 he wrote:

> The Federation will . . . unite in spirit the students of the world . . . in doing this it will be achieving a yet more significant result —the hastening of the answer to our Lord's prayer, "that they all may be one." We read and hear much about Christian union.

[3] W. H. T. Gairdner, *Echoes From Edinburgh 1910* (Westwood, N. J.: Fleming H. Revell Company, Author's Ed:), p. 64.

Surely there has been recently no more hopeful development towards the real spiritual union of Christendom than the World's Student Christian Federation which unites in common purpose and work the coming leaders of Church and State in all lands.[4]

All these are ideas that we shall find growing and broadening out through the whole course of our study. The development from Mott's international student work that was most important for the Edinburgh Conference has yet to be mentioned.

What are we to do about our denominations? As long as we live in the little world of our own church or parish, we are aware of the existence of other denominations and perhaps feel quite friendly towards them, but we do not have to bother much about our relationships with them. But the moment we begin to think about co-operation with other Christians, the problem of denominationalism raises its ugly head. Prior to the end of the nineteenth century two main solutions to the problem had been found. To some the principles of their own denomination seemed so important that it proved practically impossible for them to move out of the charmed circle into fellowship with any other group of Christians. On this side the problem of the Roman Catholic Church and its relations with other Christians will come before us later in our studies. Another approach, characteristic of the great evangelical movements of the nineteenth century, was to say that denominations really do not matter very much; the all-important thing is faith in Christ, and if we are agreed on that, we need not talk very much about the details of those things that divide us. In the task of witnessing to Christ we find ourselves completely at one.

The Student Christian Movement, as it developed, came into contact with certain groups such as High Church Anglicans and later the Orthodox churches, which really longed for fellowship but were not prepared to enter into it at the price of having to regard as unimportant those things on which the churches disagree. Could such folk come into an interchurch fellowship or could they not? Here came the new discovery. We need not think of our own denominational loyalty as an unfortunate limitation,

[4] From *A History of the Ecumenical Movement*, p. 341, by Stephen Charles Neill and Ruth Rouse. Published 1954. The Westminster Press.

about which the less said the better; we may think of it as a treasure which is to be shared with others, in so far as they are able to accept it. Students were encouraged to join the Student Movement in full loyalty to the church to which they belonged and to bring with them all the beliefs and the traditions of that church as a valuable contribution to the fulness of the Christian life within the movement. No one need deny or try to hide anything which he believed to be true, but no one must try to impose on others his own particular beliefs.

Many of the leaders in the preparations for the Edinburgh Conference were already familiar with this new principle of co-operation. It was the acceptance of this principle that made possible the presence at the Conference of certain groups which otherwise would certainly not have been there. And in particular, through this acceptance one of the most remarkable of all those who were present in Edinburgh in that month of June had felt able to accept the invitation to be present and to address the Conference.

Randall Davidson, Archbishop of Canterbury, was probably the wisest statesman that any church has produced in this century. He had a great knowledge of men and of the life of the churches. No orator, he was at his best in the House of Lords, where no one ever gives any sign of listening to what anyone else is saying, where any attempt at rhetoric is frowned on, but where a cool, reasoned presentation of a case is certain to be listened to with respect. Such was the confidence felt in Davidson by churchmen throughout the world that any action on his part carried great weight, and his willingness to bless this new international movement gave confidence to a good many people who might otherwise have been inclined to be suspicious of it. Not only so, when he spoke of the place of missions in the church, this ordinarily dull speaker seemed suddenly to catch fire and to speak with all the authority of the authentic prophetic voice:

> The place of missions in the life of the Church must be the central place and none other. . . . Secure for that thought its true place, in our plans, our policy, our prayers, and then—why then, the issue is His, not ours. But it may well be that if that come true, "there be some standing here to-night who shall

not taste of death till they see"—here on earth, in a way we know not now—"the Kingdom of God come with power."[5]

We are still far from having exhausted the ways in which this great Conference proved itself to be remarkable and prophetic.

It came just at the end of the most rapid period of development that the Christian mission had ever known since the first century. The great William Carey, who worked in Bengal from 1793 to 1834, once suggested that a general missionary conference should be held in 1810, perhaps at the Cape of Good Hope. It is interesting to contrast the one century with the other. If the conference had been held in 1810, who would have come to it? There would not have been a single soul to represent China or Japan or Korea. The heroic pioneers had begun to make their mark in the South Seas. India had her devoted band of witnesses in north and south. The Cape, Sierra Leone, the Gold Coast, a few outposts on the coast could represent Christianity in Africa, but the whole of the interior of that vast continent was still completely unknown. And now in 1910, although the Conference had before it a report on "Unoccupied Fields," it could affirm that at least the Christian claim had been staked out in almost every country in the world, and that the plans had been laid for further advance. In many ways the most difficult part of the task had been accomplished. Countless languages had been learned and in many cases for the first time reduced to writing by the missionaries themselves. The New Testament had been translated into two hundred languages. Through scientific discovery life in the tropics had been made safer and more tolerable for the white man. Many missionary methods had been tried; mistakes had been made and rectified. Above all it had been shown that the gospel is the power of God unto salvation to all the nations. Some converts had been won from every known form of human religion; few from among high-caste Hindus, Muslims, Sikhs, and Parsees, and yet those few were significant as showing that what most people, including many Christians, had deemed to be impossible had actually been done. At the other end of the scale the Eskimo, in his fastnesses of ice and snow, and the Indian outcaste had heard the gospel and had been transformed by it.

[5] *Op. cit.*, p. 150.

No wonder that the Conference met on the crest of a wave of enthusiasm and confidence.

All this had been the achievement of the Western nations. One of the fruits of missionary work had been seen among the ancient churches of the East, which had begun to awake from the somnolence that had overtaken them as the result of long centuries of Muslim domination, but so far they had made but few contributions to the expansion of the Christian church. But in this close association of missionary work with Western power a danger lay concealed only just beneath the surface. Exaggerated tales have gone round about missionaries who lent themselves to be tools in the hands of their governments for the development of political and colonial plans. In point of fact missionaries have as often been in opposition to their governments as hand in glove with them. Missions have been accused of recklessly breaking up cultures and civilizations that they did not understand and unnecessarily westernizing their converts. No doubt missionaries did make mistakes and sometimes confused the habits of their own country with the essentials of the gospel, but quite often the shoe was on the other foot. The converts grasped eagerly at everything that came from the West, suitable or unsuitable. Do not African gentlemen still go to church on Sunday mornings in the sweltering heat of West Africa, in thick European tweed suits? Quite often it was the missionary who encouraged his people to keep some of the harmless and useful customs that were their inheritance. Yet when every attempt has been made to keep the balance, it is just the fact that the great age of missionary expansion was also the great age of colonialism. It was to be feared that, if a reaction against the West and all its ways were to set in, a great deal of Christian work would be liable to be swept away in the reaction.

To the perceptive signs were not lacking that the great change might already be on the way. In 1905 Japan had defeated Russia. Russia was only marginally a Western power. Yet here was the new phenomenon of one of the ancient nations of the East, waking up from centuries of sleep and in fifty years raising itself to a level at which it was accepted by the whole of the West as a first-class military power. The physical impregnability of the West had been successfully challenged. Its moral superiority was next, and very shortly, to be called in question. When in 1914 the "Christian nations" set to fighting one another and to drawing millions of non-Christians into their quarrel, they destroyed for good and all the myth of the Christian West; all that their successors in 1939 had to do was to stamp on the few remaining fragments of Western reputation. After 1910 the Christian missionary cause was never again to speak in accents of such triumphant confidence and forward-looking hope.

Edinburgh 1910 was specifically a *missionary* conference. Of the more than 1,200 men and women who came together, only eighteen were from the younger churches, and not one, even of those few, had come as representative of a church. But the delegates were well aware that, through the blessing of God on their work, churches were coming into existence in every part of the world. No subject was more earnestly discussed than the future of "the native churches." And now for the first time, and perhaps with pained surprise, the leaders of the Western churches were to find that the younger churches were beginning to be able to talk back. Among the addresses which attracted most attention was that of V. S. Azariah of India on "The problem of co-operation between foreign and native workers." Thirty-six years old at the time, Azariah was almost unknown outside India, but many of those who heard him on June 20, 1910 must have forecast something of that great career to which reference will have to be made again and again in this book. Azariah started with a plain and blunt statement:

> My personal observation . . . has revealed to me the fact that the relationship between the European missionaries and the Indian workers is far from what it ought to be and that a certain aloofness, a lack of mutual understanding and openness, a great lack of frank intercourse and friendliness, exists throughout the country.[6]

After considering why this might be so and suggesting various steps that ought to be taken, he ended with words which rang across the world:

[6] *Op. cit.*, p. 307.

Through all the ages to come the Indian Church will rise up in gratitude to attest the heroism and self-denying labours of the missionary body. You have given your goods to feed the poor. You have given your bodies to be burned. We also ask for *love*. Give us *FRIENDS*.[7]

But we still have not come to the most important thing of all.

It must seem well-nigh incredible to readers of this book in 1960 that fifty years ago there was not in existence anywhere in the Christian world, outside Rome itself, any permanent organization charged with the work of promoting Christian international and interchurch co-operation. Each of the preceding missionary conferences had come into being almost by chance; none had taken any steps to perpetuate itself, though it was generally assumed at the end of every conference that another one would take place sometime somewhere. It was given to Edinburgh 1910 to take the first cautious step forward and to form that first slender organization out of which was to grow, in God's providence, the whole of the great world-wide ecumenical movement.

The first step was very small, and it was taken very cautiously. It is not hard to see why this was so—the same problem pursues all ecumenical action. Churches, like states, are very jealous of their independent sovereignty and autonomy. But how can you honestly go into an international movement without losing some of that autonomy? And if you allow an international organ, however modest, to come into existence, will it not tend to grow and develop until, like the fabled lion, it turns and devours its own parents? If we plant a very small acorn of co-operation in Edinburgh, will it not have grown in a few years into the spreading oak of a Protestant Vatican? And if we commit ourselves to co-operation, shall we not be led on step by step into a unity which will be a betrayal of all our denominational principles? So men thought—and think, and so the basic challenge to ecumenical advance was delivered.

It is hard to imagine a smaller acorn than that which was presented by the leaders to the Edinburgh Conference in 1910.

[7] *Op. cit.*, p. 315. The large capitals are there in the sober pages of the official report.

All that was proposed was that a Continuation Committee should be formed to carry forward the work of the Conference. To it would be assigned such modest duties as "(3) To consider when a further World Missionary Conference is desirable and to make the initial preparations." But the sting, if that is the right word for it, lay in number six: "To confer with the Societies and Boards as to the best method of working towards the formation of . . . a permanent International Missionary Committee." This had in it the promise of as yet undefined possibilities; though once again the note of caution is sounded in the remark that, if such a committee come into being, "it should be a purely consultative and advisory Association, exercising no authority but such as would accrue to it through the intrinsic value of the services that it may be able to render."

"The motion is carried unanimously." As the chairman made the announcement, the great assembly rose spontaneously to its feet and sang the Doxology. Those who were present knew that something great had happened. They could not foresee how their acorn would grow nor on how great a tree the few survivors would look out, when fifty years on they came to observe the jubilee of the day of sowing.

The Continuation Committee was formed. Perhaps the most important thing about it was the three names with which the list of its membership was closed:

FROM JAPAN
Bishop Honda

FROM CHINA
Mr. Cheng Ching-yi

FROM INDIA
The Rev. Dr. Chatterji

The right of the younger churches to be heard and to be represented by their own people had been unmistakably recognized.

The Continuation Committee met immediately after the end of the Conference. Almost inevitably the first sentence of its record reads: "It elected Dr. John R. Mott as Chairman." So

John R. Mott took up a burden that he was not to lay down for nearly forty years.[8]

Perhaps Mott himself had foreseen something of the vocation that would come to him, as to others, as the outcome of the Conference. This chapter cannot more fitly close than with a few sentences of his closing address:

> The end of the Conference is the beginning of the conquest. The end of the planning is the beginning of the doing. What shall be the issue of these memorable days? . . . These and other things that press upon the whole emotional and mental nature of the delegates constitute our undoing and our peril if they issue not in performance. If these things do not move everyone of us, if these things do not move us to enter with Christ into larger things, I ask it reverently, what can the living God do that will move us? . . . It may be that the words of the Archbishop shall prove to be a splendid prophecy, and that before many of us taste death we shall see the Kingdom of God come with power.[9]

[8] During the Conference the University of Edinburgh had conferred on him the degree of Honorary Doctor of Law—the first of the innumerable doctorates that were to be showered upon him.

[9] *World Missionary Conference: History, Records and Addresses*, pp. 347, 349, 351.

II

Nathan Soederblom and Life and Work

ACCORDING TO THE LAW OF SWEDEN, THE FINAL WORD IN THE appointment of an archbishop of Uppsala rests with the king. Three names are sent forward to him, but he has complete liberty in choosing the one among the three whom he regards as best fitted for this high office. In 1914 the archbishopric was vacant; passing over the first two names on the list, King Gustav V gave his decision in favor of the third. And so at the age of 48 Nathan Soederblom became the chief pastor of the church of his native land.

Few among ecumenical leaders have had so thorough and international a training as Soederblom. He was born not far from the Arctic circle in the home of a poor country parson. There he learned much of the way in which ordinary people live, of the trials and sorrows that come to poor folk under the stress of a harsh and ungracious climate. After a brilliant career as a student at Uppsala he went to be pastor of the Swedish church in Paris and at the same time chaplain to seamen. During his student days, he had paid a visit to America for the Northfield Student Conference; this had brought him into contact with the young leadership of the Student Movements of the world and had added to the deep evangelical piety he had learned in his father's home and to his interest in missionary work a sense of international Christianity and of the possibilities for Christian unity in his day. At this conference he wrote in his diary: "Lord, give me humility and wisdom to serve the great cause of the free unity of thy church."

Soederblom's main activity as a student had been in the field of the history of religions. After some years as a professor in his own university he had added to this responsibility that of professor of the history of religions at Leipzig in Germany. He was actually there when the news of his election to the archbishopric reached him. Perfectly at home in Swedish, French, and German, and with a good knowledge of English, widely read in the literature and theology of many nations, he seemed just the man to lead his church out into the forefront of ecumenical and international activity.

The hour was matched with the man. Hardly had Soederblom taken up his new office when the tornado of the First World War burst upon the nations. We are now so used to one war after another and to a cold war which seems destined to go on without end that it is hard for us to realize the shock and horror caused to the peoples of all civilized countries by this return to the law of the jungle, and by the abandonment of the progress that had been gained in centuries of peaceful intercourse. It was always recognized that war might continue to occur in less advanced parts of the world—Italians might fight Turks, and the Balkin countries were in a state of perpetual effervescence. Thoughtful people had for some time been aware of increasing tension among the great nations of Europe. But it was the general opinion that in the twentieth century war just could not happen. Now it had happened, and dreams had to be exchanged for the harshest and cruelest realities.

Sweden was a neutral country. Soederblom felt to the full the horror of the situation into which the nations of Europe had been plunged. It seemed to him his God-given duty to call the leaders of the churches to joint action in order that as soon as possible the destruction and bloodshed might cease and peace come back to a troubled world. So in November 1914 he sent out to a great many church leaders in many countries, with the request that they would sign it, a statement that he had drawn up under the title "For Peace and Christian Fellowship":

The war is causing untold distress. Christ's body, the Church, suffers and mourns. Mankind in its need cries out, O Lord, how long? . . . We servants of the Church, address to all those who have power or influence in the matter an earnest appeal seriously to keep peace before their eyes, in order that bloodshed soon may cease. . . . Our Faith perceives what the eye cannot always see: the strife of nations must finally serve the dispensation of the Almighty, and all the faithful in Christ are one. Let us therefore call upon God that he may destroy hate and enmity, and in mercy ordain peace for us. His will be done! [1]

Soederblom was disappointed that so few of the leaders to whom he wrote were willing to sign his manifesto. The sentiments to which he had given expression were unexceptionable. But had he taken into account all the difficulties of the situation? The Germans were convinced that they were an innocent people, bravely resisting an unprovoked attack made on them by powerful enemies. To the rest of the world events presented themselves in a very different light. Germany had violated her own pledged word to respect the neutrality of Belgium. Fair and rich provinces of France had been occupied by German armies. In May 1915 the sinking of the Lusitania shocked the conscience of the world. Yet from Uppsala came no word of condemnation of these and other crimes. Had the Swedish Archbishop really understood the situation? He knew Germany well, understood the German point of view, and was valued by the German government for his "honest friendship for Germany." He had far less acquaintance with England; America he never really came to understand at all. It was not unnatural that those who were deeply committed to a cause, as all patriotic citizens must be in time of war, looked with uncertainty on these well-meant efforts by a neutral to promote the cause of peace and felt that, terrible as war must be, the rejection of the moral principles on which European civilization has been built up might in the end be more terrible still. So for the moment little if anything came of Soederblom's efforts.

Yet the vision did not fade. In one crisis the churches had failed to maintain peace. Were they destined to remain for ever in that same impotence? They had failed to act together when the clouds of war were gathering. Could they learn to work together in times of peace and so to prepare for greater effectiveness if if another crisis were to burst suddenly upon the nations? It

[1] Text in Swedish, German, English, and French in N. Karlstroem: *Kristna Samforstandsstravanden under Varldskriget 1914-1918* (Stockholm, 1947) pp. 578-80.

was the business of the churches to prepare men for an eternal destiny. Had they no concern for the conditions under which men live in this life, no moral responsibility for decision in matters of politics and economics and of the social order?

Gradually, thoughts took shape, and Soederblom saw the vision of an ecumenical meeting in which the divided churches of Christendom would come together, not like the councils of old to define dark and mysterious doctrines of the faith, but to discuss frankly together the urgent problems of practical Christianity. He had failed to mobilize the leaders of the churches in time of war; now he would set to work to bring them together in the days of peace.

In the life of Randall Davidson, Archbishop of Canterbury, there is a delightful description of the first meeting, in May 1921, between Davidson and the Archbishop of Uppsala. The character of the two men is perfectly set out in the account of this affair. Davidson was, before all else, a wise and prudent ecclesiastical statesman, and nothing could shake his inveterate Scottish shrewdness and caution. Soederblom was the enthusiast, accustomed to making light of difficulties and to believing that things would happen just because he willed them to happen. A list of subjects that the two Archbishops might like to discuss had been drawn up by the chaplain. Soederblom happened to light on this paper in the chaplain's study, added one or two items to the list, and changed the order, putting "Universal Conference on Life and Work" at the top of the list. When this was reported to Davidson, he smiled and said, "He is a dangerous man." Diplomatic conversation proceeded for half an hour; the Archbishop of Uppsala always trying to edge it round to the proposed conference, the Archbishop of Canterbury always mysteriously managing to steer it on to some other urgent topic. At last Soederblom managed to get ten minutes on the conference, but even then Davidson was not to be drawn:

He did not obtain a clear opinion about the Conference from the Archbishop of Canterbury, who was unwilling to give himself away, either for or against, and had previously told his chaplain that he hoped he would not be asked for a definite answer, but if he were asked would say that he would consult the Archbishop of York.[2]

This meeting between two of the most remarkable churchmen of modern times is interesting in itself, but it has been recorded here at some length because it is typical of the difficulties which Soederblom had to face in every direction. Church leaders are necessarily prudent people and do not wish to be led into adventures which may in the end prove unfruitful, if not embarrassing. There were no precedents for what Soederblom was proposing. The Edinburgh Conference had indeed met, but that was an unofficial gathering of interested people to consider one aspect, and that on the whole an uncontroversial aspect, of the life of the church. Now something far grander was being planned —a meeting to which the churches as such would give their blessing, to which they would send official representatives charged with the task of discussing some of the most explosive subjects in the world. It is not surprising that many hesitated, convinced either that the meeting would not be held at all, or that if held it might prove to be more of a danger than a consolation to the churches.

But Soederblom had grounds for confidence. He was far from being the only Christian to feel that the war had represented a fearful abdication of their responsibility on the part of the churches. The sense of Christian social responsibility had been slowly but steadily growing in many parts of the world. It no longer seemed sufficient that the churches should preach a gospel of individual salvation; their voice should be heard in those areas of confusion and perplexity which were the legacy of the industrial revolution and of the domination established by the white races over nearly three-quarters of the population of the world. In England the great prophet had been F. D. Maurice, who had challenged the accepted philosophy and economics of his day and had affirmed that co-operation is a more effective principle than the unlimited competition which in his day was held to be necessary in industrial affairs. His

[2] G. K. A. Bell, *Randall Davidson* (London: Oxford University Press, 3rd. ed., 1952), pp. 1049-51. (The chaplain concerned in this affair was named G. K. A. Bell!)

thought continued to work in the minds of disciples, both within and outside the Church of England, and led in 1911 to the formation of the Interdenominational Social Service Council. Similar movements came into being in France, in Germany, and in Switzerland. In America the Social Gospel, of which Walter Rauschenbusch and Francis G. Peabody were the most noted prophets, had laid down the principle that the whole life of society must be penetrated by the spirit of Christianity. One of the first actions of the Federal Council of the Churches of Christ in America was its adoption in 1908 of "the Social Creed of the Churches." On the basis of such thought and such concern Soederblom was able to build his great design.

It was in England that action was first taken to give clear expression to the post-war concern for the practical application of Christian principles. Quite independently of Soederblom and his plans, a number of English church leaders had decided, as early as 1921, to convene a great conference on Christian Politics, Economics and Citizenship—the very terms, familiar as they may now seem, sounded paradoxical at the time of their enunciation. The basis of the Conference was expressed as follows:

> The basis of this Conference is the conviction that the Christian Faith, rightly interpreted and consistently followed, gives the vision and the power essential for solving the problems of today, that the social ethics of Christianity have been greatly neglected by Christians with disastrous consequences to the individual and to society, and that it is of the first importance that these should be given a clearer and more persistent emphasis.[3]

Very careful preparations were made. Twelve commissions met over a long period of time to discuss such subjects as education, the treatment of crime, the Christian attitude to war and peace. Many of the best brains in the country lent their co-operation, and this ecumenical enterprise was distinguished by the fact that many leading Roman Catholics took part in the studies, until at a late stage disagreement on certain matters of principle led to their withdrawal. Unlike many ecumenical publica-

[3] *The Proceedings of C.O.P.E.C.* (London: Longmans, 1924), p. xi.

tions, the "COPEC" reports proved immediately popular; a number of them had to be reprinted three times within a year of their first appearance. Their up-to-date and relevant character may be illustrated by a single quotation from the report on peace and war: "The future destiny of mankind cannot be determined by Europe and America; Asia and Africa will become of increasing importance."

It has to be admitted that the Conference itself, held at Birmingham April 5-12, 1924, was rather dull. No one has yet solved the problem of what is to be done with these very large and miscellaneous gatherings of Christians, most of whom have not had time to read the literature prepared for their edification. Such numbers of people cannot possibly engage in profitable debate or discussion. And yet such an assembly becomes deeply discontented if it becomes too clear that the members have been brought together only to serve as a rubber stamp for decisions already reached by their devoted and hard-working committees. The problem is still with us and seems likely to remain unsolved till the end of time.

Still, there were some striking moments in the Conference. One came right at the start, when the chairman, William Temple, at that time Bishop of Manchester, defined what he believed the purpose of the Conference to be:

> The fundamental aim of the Conference is that we may receive a new realisation of God, especially in relation to those phases of life from which any direct reference to God has usually of late been excluded.

This puts it all in a nutshell; is there any phase of life from which God and the law of Christ can be excluded? The man of the world answers "many." The ecumenically-minded Christian answers "none."

Then there was the moment at which the Archbishop of Uppsala, at that time almost unknown in Britain, addressed the Conference on the proposed World Conference on Life and Work.

> He would make three points. (1) He commended the admirable reports. (2) The Conference had shortened the way between faith and action. The way was perhaps shorter for English and

American Churches than for others. (3) Copec has made Christians uncomfortable, and that is often the best service that can be given to a man.[4]

In the meantime preparations were going forward in Sweden and elsewhere, and at last the great day arrived. On August 19, 1925 the Universal Christian Conference on Life and Work, made up of more than five hundred representatives from thirty-seven nations, convened in Stockholm. Its aim:

Without entering into questions of Faith and Order . . . to unite the different Churches in common practical work, to furnish the Christian conscience with an organ of expression in the midst of the great spiritual movements of our time, and to insist that the principles of the Gospel be applied to the solution of contemporary social and international problems.[5]

It is impossible to exaggerate the part played in the conference by Archbishop Soederblom. Without attempting unduly to impress his personality on the proceedings, he was everywhere and in everything, alert, adroit, patient. Sixty years old, he had brought to the Conference all the fruits of a many-sided experience of the church, of watchful hope and expectation, of a resolution to see this Conference through that could not be dimmed or dulled by apathy, criticism, or hostility on the part of others. One observer has described how, welcoming a group of guests no two of whom could speak the same language, he would dart from one to the other, slipping with perfect ease from one tongue to another, bringing all together and making all feel at home in one fellowship. His fellow-Swede Nils Ehrenstroem has written penetratingly that "an authentic and indispensable touch was his great sense of humour and his amazing faculty of creating around him an atmosphere of joyous festivity. But it was a humour glittering over mysterious depths; it is suggestive that his sympathetic study of Luther carries the title *Humour and Melancholy.*"[6] And Miss Lucy Gardner, one

[4] *The Proceedings of C.O.P.E.C.*, p. 261.
[5] *The Stockholm Conference 1925* (ed. G. K. A. Bell, Oxford University Press, 1926), p. i.
[6] Rouse & Neill, *op. cit.*, p. 546.

of the secretaries of COPEC, used of him a word which only rarely finds its way into the solemn records of ecumenical debate:

I hardly dare begin to speak of the beloved President—in fact, I am not sure that he comes, so to speak, within my terms of reference—or indeed that he even comes within anybody's terms of reference. But I will just say that we have grown to love him and that the memory of his great vision—his *fun* and his spiritual understanding, will always be very precious.[7]

Hardly less remarkable than Soederblom was the secretary of the Conference, the newly appointed Dean of Canterbury, George Bell. Forty-one years old, but looking much younger than his years, Bell, after a brilliant career as student and teacher at Oxford, had gone to be chaplain to Archbishop Davidson. We have already noted Davidson's personal greatness. But beyond this he had a capacity, unequalled by any other Christian leader of this century, for producing greatness in others. It was his habit to gather able young men round him as his chaplains, to discern their special gifts, to trust them with important responsibilities, and so to send out into the church as leaders men of sterling quality and tested intelligence. So Bell came to the conference with ten years' experience of dealing with great affairs in church and state. Modest, reserved, simple almost to the point of naivete, unaffectedly devout, Bell was incapable of seeking anything for himself. He had an abiding concern for the unity of Christ's people upon earth and for the manifestation of Christ's rule in every part of the life of men and nations. He did not seek greatness, but greatness was thrust upon him. And when he died in 1958, the whole Christian world mourned for one of whom it could be said, as of an earlier servant of God, that "he was a good man and feared God above many."

The Conference had hardly opened before it ran into stormy waters. What do we mean by the kingdom of God, and what share has man in bringing it to accomplishment?

The opening sermon was preached by Frank Theodore Woods, Bishop of Winchester, who had won a high reputation in Britain

[7] *The Stockholm Conference 1925* (Ed. G. K. A. Bell, London: Oxford University Press, 1926), p. 737.

as an expert on social and industrial problems. He started off in terms of considerable optimism: "We believe in the kingdom of Heaven. We are conspirators for its establishment. That is why we are here. That is the meaning of this Conference." And towards the end of the sermon he struck the same note again:

To set up the Kingdom of God in this complicated civilization of the twentieth century is a colossal task, a task which demands thought, skill, patience, wisdom. But, I repeat, in Christ we can do the impossible. Therefore, in this opening act of worship we do our homage to Him.[8]

It was almost inevitable that this British optimism should be met by a sharp challenge, almost a rebuke, from another side, and this happened in the allocution of His Magnificence the Bishop of Saxony, Dr. Ihmels.

It is nothing but self-deception to suppose that the Kingdom of God will reach its perfect development in this age. . . . Nothing could be more mistaken or more disastrous than to suppose that we mortal men have to build up God's kingdom in this world. We must be careful how we express this. We can do nothing, we have nothing, we are nothing.[9]

Here we find two points of view that have remained locked in apparently inextricable opposition all through the ecumenical history of fifty years. It may serve a useful purpose to put them in their extreme form. On the one hand some Christians have sincerely believed that God has millenniums and ages in which to work out his purpose, and that one day the kingdom of God will certainly be established on this earth. It is man's task to work with God for the manifestation of that kingdom. It is true that without Christ we can do nothing, but with him we can do all things and work with full confidence in the blessing of God upon our work. On the other hand other Christians equally sincere have affirmed that the kingdom is always the gift of God which comes down from above; it is never the work of man. It will appear only at the end of the ages when Christ

[8] *Ibid.*, p. 45.
[9] *Ibid.*, pp. 75, 76.

comes again in glory. All human hopes may be frustrated, and all human effort is based on sand. The German looks with pained contempt on the naive optimism of the American, who confuses the kingdom of God with the American way of life and steadily refuses to face the elements of evil and destruction that exist in human life. The American looks with sad contempt on the continental, who supposes that the putting out of some of his own lights of hope is identical with the extinction of the sun and all the stars and is prepared to sit with folded hands awaiting the trump of doom and the end of all earthly things. Nearly thirty years later the preparations for the Evanston Assembly of 1954 showed that the old misunderstandings were as much alive as ever; we have not yet reached the point at which these diverse understandings of the Christian hope are complementary rather than contradictory.

In twelve days the Conference made a rapid tour, under the guidance of experts, of all those areas in the life of men on which the church has so often failed to speak and on which it was the conviction of the majority of the delegates that it ought now to speak with insight and courage. At the end the Conference launched its message, its only official statement, a document only six pages long and of exemplary simplicity, modesty, and humility:

The Conference has deepened and purified our devotion to the Captain of our Salvation. Responding to His call, "Follow Me," we have in the presence of the Cross accepted the urgent duty of applying His Gospel in all realms of human life—industrial, social, political and international. . . . Only as we become inwardly one shall we attain real unity of mind and spirit. The nearer we draw to the Crucified, the nearer we come to one another, in however varied colours the Light of the World may be reflected in our faith. Under the Cross of Jesus Christ we reach out hands to one another. The Good Shepherd had to die in order that He might gather together the scattered children of God. In the Crucified and Risen Lord alone lies the world's hope.[10]

[10] *Ibid.* pp. 711, 715-16.

Many had believed that the Conference could never take place. It had taken place. It had met and talked and prayed and dispersed. What was left, now that it was over?

In the first place Stockholm 1925 was a great and representative assembly. Not so many peoples were represented as at Edinburgh 1910. But this time the Orthodox churches of the East were present with a delegation of nineteen, including such well-known figures as Archbishop Germanos of Thyateira and Dr. Alivisatos of the University of Athens. One of the most impressive moments in the Conference had been the recitation of the Nicene Creed in Greek, at the closing service, by Photios, Patriarch and Pope of Alexandria. The greatest weakness was on the side of the younger churches; only six nationals were present from China, Japan, and India, apparently no one at all from Africa.

What is even more important is that the majority of those present had been formally appointed by their churches. We are moving out of the period in which ecumenical activity was the chosen vocation of individuals; slowly and almost unaware, the churches themselves are being led into responsibility, and the church period of the ecumenical movement is beginning.

The Conference had revealed many differences of opinion, both on theological and on practical questions. It had not entirely bridged the gulf that still separated the Germans from the representatives of the other European nations. Yet for almost all the delegates these had been days of illumination. Across the barriers of confession, race, and language Christians were discovering one another and finding that those things which unite us in Christ are immensely more important than those things that divide.

Most important of all, Stockholm 1925 like Edinburgh 1910 felt that it had begun a great work that must be carried forward. A Continuation Committee of forty-five members was appointed. This was a disappointment to some, who had hoped to see the creation of some permanent organization more grandiose in form and impressive in title. But probably it was wise in 1925 to take only cautious steps forward. Much that we now take for granted was in those days regarded as rash and venturesome; the churches had to be gradually persuaded that they were not signing away their own independence by taking part in international Christian work. So the duties of the Continuation Committee were defined in rather stringent and restrictive terms, and it was emphatically laid down that the Committee should "have no power to speak in the name or on behalf of the Churches or to take any action that shall commit any Church, its deliverances being simply its own opinion, unless any particular deliverance or deliverances shall be expressly approved by the Church or Churches concerned." These sensible limitations apply to all the organs of ecumenical activity; they do not impede freedom of study and action over a wide range of human and Christian concerns.

So Life and Work was born. The feet of the churches had been firmly set on the path that was to lead to Oxford 1937, to Amsterdam 1948, to Evanston 1954, and to that undisclosed future which still belongs to the realm of prophecy and not to that of history.

III

Charles Brent and Faith and Order

FAITH AND ORDER. TO MANY CHURCHMEN THESE WORDS HAD AN almost menacing ring. Two great international Christian conferences had been held, and from the proceedings of each of them the consideration of questions of faith and order had been specifically excluded. This seemed quite reasonable at the time. The missionary proclamation of the gospel is a practical business and does not necessarily demand that its supporters should work backwards from practice to theory. The concern of Stockholm was with ''practical Christianity'' (and in German this became the official name of the movement that in English was known as ''Life and Work''). Almost with relief Christians had come to believe that in practical service they could find the solvent for agelong differences; ''Service unites, doctrine divides'' was a slogan much heard in those days.

Yet is the matter one which can be settled quite so easily as that? Christians go to the non-Christian lands to preach the gospel. But what gospel is it that they go to preach? Can this question be considered without bringing in all kinds of questions of faith and theology? And how are we to explain, or explain away, to the non-Christian world the hundred or more missionary organizations that are at work in India? As we have seen, on the very first day Stockholm 1925 stumbled on grave theological divergences. Up to a certain point we can say that such divergences are no part of our immediate concern, but how far can we really act together, if there are undisclosed differences of conviction, unresolved contradictions in our way of getting at things? Questions of faith and order may be postponed; they cannot forever be evaded.

This was the vision that came to one of the delegates to the Edinburgh Conference of 1910. We ought not to be afraid of these questions; precisely at their points of difference Christians ought to be able to meet in humility and frankness, to speak with one another in love, and to find a way through. God has laid on the churches immense new tasks; in their separation they must needs be weak; only in union can they find the strength for the work that God has given them to do. "I was converted," he wrote. "I learned that something was working that was not of man in that conference; that the Spirit of God . . . was preparing a new era in the history of Christianity." The writer of these words was Charles Henry Brent, missionary bishop in the Philippines of the Protestant Episcopal Church in the United States of America.

Among all the figures that pass across the ecumenical stage, none is more attractive than that of this son of a Canadian parsonage who became a great apostle of Christian unity. After ten years' work in a city mission in Boston Brent was appointed in 1901 to the pioneer job of bishop in the Philippines, which had but recently come under American control. There was an immediate influx of American Protestant missions, most of which gave themselves to the comparatively easy task of detaching nominal or discontented members from the Church of Rome, to which eighty per cent or more of the population belonged. While not absolutely refusing to countenance such work, Brent felt that a mission should be primarily a mission to the non-Christians; so from the start he directed the energies of the Episcopalians far inland and into the mountains of northern Luzon, where lived simple people untouched by the gospel and accessible to those who would approach them with endless patience and endurance of hardship. The seal was set on this side of Brent's work, when in 1959 for the first time a Filipino priest was consecrated to the high office of suffragan bishop of the missionary district which Brent had founded.

Brent was one of those men who cannot long remain hidden. Much of his work was quiet and obscure. But he became the friend and confidant of successive governors of the Philippines, and through one of them he was brought into international prominence as president of the first International Opium Commission held at Shanghai. His strength of understanding and integrity of judgment commended him to laymen concerned with these delicate matters of international law and action.

On those who met him casually or in public, Brent always left an impression of strength and decision. His diaries reveal another and unexpected side of the man. He was at times bowed down by an almost morbid sense of failure and unworthiness. If he manifested strength and wisdom, he would have attributed this humbly to the power of Christ, which is made perfect in weakness, and to the wisdom of Christ, which can take the foolish things of the world and make them wise. More than almost any other ecumenical leader Brent had learned the secret of the hidden life of the soul in God; this was his life, and without it he would have found it impossible to serve. Whenever possible he liked to spend the hour between 6:00 and 7:00 A.M. in meditation and to follow this with half an hour for prayer and an hour for study. It was his habit to write down his prayers; we shall make use of two of them as the concluding words of this chapter.

Such was the man who, at the age of forty-eight, felt himself possessed by a new vision and a new call at the Edinburgh Conference of 1910. He lost no time in making others aware of the thoughts that were stirring in his mind. The General Convention of the American Episcopal Church was to meet in October, 1910. On the day before its opening Brent addressed a large public meeting; he spoke of his conviction that God was in a new way calling the churches to unity and expressed the opinion that the time had come for the churches frankly to examine their differences in a "world conference on faith and order." This was probably the first occasion on which these prophetic words were used. Many agreed that something must be done. At the General Convention a resolution was proposed by W. T. Manning, later bishop of New York, and unanimously accepted, to the effect that

> A Joint Commission be appointed to bring about a Conference for the consideration of questions touching Faith and Order, and that all Christian Communions throughout the world which confess our Lord Jesus Christ as God and Saviour be asked to unite with us in arranging for and conducting such a conference.[1]

[1] Rouse and Neill, *op. cit.*, p. 407.

Faith and Order had been born.

So much has happened in fifty years that it is almost impossible for Christians of the younger generation to realise how revolutionary this proposal was at the time at which it was made. If you have never lived without electricity and the telephone, it is almost impossible to imagine a world in which these elementary conveniences do not exist. If you have grown up in the modern atmosphere of international Christianity, it is hard to picture the endless labors and patience of the pioneers, by whom things that we take for granted today were gradually brought into the common Christian consciousness. In 1910 a great many Christian leaders regarded the holding of such a Christian conference as first impossible, and secondly undesirable. As one leader pungently remarked, "If they do meet, they will do nothing but quarrel, and make things worse than they were before. They had far better stay at home." Scholars recalled with apprehension the atmosphere which prevailed at some of the early councils, when the more precise definition of the faith was couched in the terms of bitter anathemas, and the final result was exclusion and division rather than the healing of the breaches in the Christian world. No such conference had ever been held in modern times; there was no certainty that the churches would respond or that a meeting of any significance would take place. Unless Brent and his colleagues had been men of rock-like faith, they would certainly have fainted and failed under the sheer weight of the difficulties that had to be faced and overcome.

It was fortunate that Brent was not alone in his convictions. To his aid, though at first only indirectly, came Peter Ainslie of the Disciples of Christ. The Disciples had been brought into existence in the early years of the nineteenth century for one single purpose—to recall the churches to New Testament Christianity, and thus to bring them back to the unity which they ought never to have lost. But as has so often happened in Christian history, a great movement for unity lost its impetus and took on the form of just one more of the endless denominations into which the church of Christ is divided. Peter Ainslie felt it to be his vocation to call the Disciples back to that activity on behalf of Christian union, which was the sole reason for their existence. In the years following 1910 he brought into being the Association for the Promotion of Christian Unity, of which he became president, and in 1911 launched the *Christian Union Quarterly,* an open forum for the discussion of all questions related to Christian union, which he edited until his death in 1934.

Even more remarkable was the long association between Brent and Robert Hallowell Gardiner, the layman who had become secretary of the Commission of the Episcopal Church. Inevitably Faith and Order has been a clerical movement; much of its work has been in the hands of the theological experts, who alone can walk with confidence in the midst of the highly technical questions that have constantly to be dealt with. It must not be forgotten that the man who gave shape and form to Brent's vision was a layman and a lawyer.

The two men were an admirable team. To Brent was given the vision of the prophet and the gift of expressing in biting and vigorous language the challenge. Behind him, usually in the shadow, was Gardiner, always ready to bring to a knotty problem his keen, legally trained mind, and eager to work out the details of such organization as was necessary to realize the vision of his colleague.[2]

"Well, this means business." Such was the remark of some friends of the movement, when in 1913 they saw the names of the committee appointed on behalf of the Church of England by the Archbishops of Canterbury and York to co-operate with the American movement.[3] The same, or almost the same, words must have come spontaneously into the mind of everyone who had to do with Gardiner. He believed in getting things done and in getting them done without delay. Two great weapons formed his armory—the pamphlet and the letter. Almost from the start, quietly and unobtrusively, the series of Faith and Order Pamphlets began to make their way into the world. None carried any authority other than that of the Commission of the Episcopal Church. Some were requests for prayer, others reports of con-

[2] A. C. Zabriskie, *Bishop Brent* (Philadelphia: The Westminster Press, 1948), p. 149.

[3] *Faith and Order Pamphlet,* no. 24, p. 9.

ferences, others serious theological documents. The following note indicates the international character which the work had taken on from the start:

4. Leaflet no. 2 in Modern Greek
5. Leaflet no. 2 in Latin
6. Leaflet no. 2 in Italian
7. Leaflet no. 2 in Russian
8. Leaflet no. 2 in German
9. Leaflet no. 2 in French
10. Leaflet no. 2 in Dutch.[4]

By 1948 the series had run up to 103 numbers, and then a new series was begun. It is typical of the modesty and simplicity of the work carried out by Gardiner that several of the pamphlets were allowed to run out to the very last copy, and no complete collection of them exists anywhere in the world.

Helped by a generous gift from J. Pierpont Morgan, Gardiner began to correspond with church leaders in all parts of the world. In an extraordinary way he managed to instil confidence into the minds of people whom he had never met, and this network of letters passing to and fro between America and almost every country in the world was the warp on which the web of Faith and Order was later to be well and truly woven. Alas, for the delays and disappointments of human affairs! Many ecumenical laborers, like Moses on Mount Pisgah, have seen the promised land from afar and have not entered into it. The first World Conference on Faith and Order did not take place till 1927; in 1924 Gardiner had been called to his rest. The Conference did well to pay glowing tribute to his work:

> Now that we can take measure of him as never before we discover him to be one of the foremost leaders and inspirers of our day. Without his sort, hope would wither, faith decline and love grow cold. There is an ache in our hearts and a void in our fellowship which must abide. And yet all the while we rejoice that the Church raises up such men to enrich and inspire mankind.[5]

[4] *Faith and Order Pamphlet,* no. 23, p. 21.

[5] *Faith and Order* Proceedings of the World Conference *Lausanne* August 3-12, *1927* (Ed. H. N. Bate, New York: George N. Doran Company, 1927) p. 12.

One other form of preparation (in which Gardiner did not take part) remains to be noted—the ecumenical pilgrimage. Delegations of churchmen, mostly American, travelled round the world to meet church leaders personally and to interest them in the proposed conference. This naturally raised the question of the limits to which they should go in planning their visitations. The answer was that there were no limits, other than that laid down in the first declaration of the purpose of the Conference, to unite all those churches which confess faith in Jesus Christ our Lord as God and Savior. This famous phrase was first used by the Young Men's Christian Association at its Paris Conference of 1855; it has passed into history as the basis of the World Council of Churches. Taken seriously, it necessarily meant that the Roman Catholic Church could not be excluded from the interest of the pilgrims. And so to Rome a number of them betook themselves in May 1919. This gave rise to one of the most famous of all ecumenical incidents.

They ought to have foreseen what would happen. That they did not foresee indicates that these, on the whole, wise and prudent men had for the moment yielded to that naive optimism which is one of the snares and perils of ecumenical activity. The Pope received them in person. He spoke with utmost graciousness, but as they left his presence, the visitors were handed a written statement, prepared well in advance, indicating that though the Pope felt goodwill for separated Christians who were seeking the way to unity, neither he nor his church could have anything to do with the proposed conference. We shall return again to the Roman Catholic attitude toward unity; that church holds that it has everything to teach and nothing to learn; it possesses the unity which Christ promised to the faithful and can bring others into that unity, but in the process it cannot receive anything from them. From this attitude the Vatican has never budged. Other Christians may regret this attitude; they must recognize it and take it seriously. So history cannot but regard as a little unreasonable the reaction of the Anglo-Catholic member of the deputation, the Bishop of Fond-du-lac, who, on leaving the papal presence, remained silent for some time and then raised his fist to heaven and "expressed his judgment on the

Bishop of Rome in terms more forceful than complimentary."[6]

At last the preliminaries were over, and on Wednesday, August 3, 1927 the great conference opened in Lausanne, appropriately under the presidency of Bishop Brent.

It was a wonderful ecclesiastical menagerie. A hundred and sixteen churches were represented. Apart from the regretted absence of the Church of Rome almost the whole Christian world seemed to be there. It was notable that delegates had come from no less than ten of the Orthodox churches and from four of the separated churches of the East.

Not less remarkable than the variety of the delegates was their distinction. The Anglican churches, for instance, had sent Gore, Temple, Headlam, and Palmer—Gore, regarded by many as the greatest theologian of the Church of England, and standing for a rather stiff Anglo-Catholic position; Temple, the rising star of the ecumenical world; Headlam, immensely learned, abrupt, impatient of blurred or muddled thinking and of any attempt to substitute feeling for hard thinking—"I deprecate any reference to the work of the Holy Spirit," he was once heard to say; Palmer, Bishop of Bombay, wagging his beard, sometimes using his slight stutter to lend explosive force to his utterances, and always calling his hearers back to the hard realities of the Christian situation. From Germany had come, among others, Karl Ludwig Schmidt, already well known as one of the pioneers of the "Form-criticism" of the New Testament; from Finland Aleksi Lehtonen, later to be Archbishop; from America William Adams Brown, the great teacher of Union Seminary, New York, and faithful ecumenical pioneer over nearly half a century; from Italy Ernesto Comba to represent the martyred Waldensian Church; from France Wilfred Monod, with the face of a mystic and a saint. And so the catalogue could go on, forming almost a summary of the church history of a century.

Yet there were defects in the representation. The younger churches were represented by learned and sympathetic Western leaders, but in the list of members there are to be found only four names of nationals of those churches. It was an old assembly; the ecumenical movement had not yet learned how necessary it

[6] Rouse and Neill, *op. cit.*, p. 416.

is to keep youth in mind in all its concerns and at every stage of them. And, of course, the gathering was overwhelmingly clerical. Of the hundred members appointed to the continuation committee, no less than forty-nine carried the mystic letters "D.D." after their names! Yet there were notable laymen among them too: "Professor of the History of Medicine, University of Toronto" and "Judge of the Supreme Court, Scotland" stand out pleasantly in the almost monotonous list of patriarchs, bishops, and provosts.

They met. They talked. They found it extraordinarily difficult to understand one another. It was not merely that there were difficulties of interpretation from one language into another. Even when the words used were the same, it became clear that long years and centuries of division had woven about the familiar words differences of connotation and of understanding. At times the members must have felt that they were attending a new Babel and that the attempt to reach understanding had succeeded only in producing new discord. This was the view of some unfriendly critics. One Canadian Roman Catholic journal reported that:

> From beginning to end the Conference was a sort of international exhibition of divisions and discordances which were beyond reconciliation. It was an undertaking by men to substitute a human voice for a divine voice in determining and deciding what God established the Catholic Church to determine and decide.[7]

Yet far more important than the recognition of division, which sheer honesty and sincerity imposed on the delegates, was that spirit which E. D. Soper has briefly formulated in the title of his book, *Lausanne, the Will to Understand.* These men had come together because they believed that beneath all the differences there was a real unity in Christ, that the task of the Conference was not to create a nonexistent unity, but to discover the unity that was already there and to find means by which it might come to fuller and more effective expression.

[7] Quoted in E. D. Soper, *Lausanne, the Will to Understand* (Garden City: Doubleday, Doran & Company, Inc., 1928), p. 129.

Of course, not everyone was happy. Most of the delegates had come from Protestant churches. There was in some minds a fear that statements might be issued that "Catholic" Christians would not be able to accept. Some were anxious lest, in the enthusiasm of mutual discovery and fellowship, the depth and reality of divergence might be overlooked. In any case it had to be made clear that this was a Conference and not a council of the churches empowered to make declarations by which the churches might be regarded as being bound. So, inevitably, the Conference had to take note of some independent and critical statements.

As always the Lutherans, and particularly those from Germany, felt themselves at a disadvantage. Few of them spoke English readily; they were not used to what they regarded as "Anglo-Saxon" methods of doing business. They were concerned to ensure that adequate theological consideration should be given to all the great problems before the Conference. So they handed in a statement of their own in which, among other things, they affirmed that

> The current discussions are, in large part, important and illuminating, and we desire that they may continue to the end of the Conference. But we question whether it is possible, and whether it comports with the dignity of this Conference and is worthy of Christendom, to announce at once as finalities the formulations here made on fundamental principles of faith and order. . . . Accordingly no final vote should be taken on the propositions formulated here. They should be added to the proclamation as material for further consideration.[8]

The Orthodox delegates also found themselves in a state of considerable bewilderment. Few of them spoke any Western language; they had never previously taken part in any such discussions with members of other churches. Sincerely committed to the cause of Christian union, they had very clear ideas as to how such union could be brought about, "only on the basis of the common confession of the ancient undivided Church of the seven Ecumenical Councils and of the first eight centuries." Again and again assurances had been given them that the purpose of

[8] *Faith and Order* (ed. H. N. Bate), p. 374.

the Conference was not to prepare a basis for immediate union of churches. Still they were apprehensive as to the meaning that might be attached to their assent to documents that they could not be certain of having fully understood. And so they declared that, while they were prepared to sign the report on the "Message of the Church," they did not feel able to sign any of the other reports, which seemed to them to have been drafted on "a basis of compromise between what in our understanding are conflicting ideas and meanings, in order to arrive at an external agreement in the letter alone."

In view of these and many other tensions it is perhaps surprising that the Conference managed to agree on anything at all. Yet it did pass six reports and handed on a seventh for further consideration by its continuation committee. The most striking and moving of the reports was naturally the first, on "The Call to Unity"; and here special attention must be drawn to the evident link between Edinburgh 1910 and Lausanne 1927:

God wills unity. Our presence in this Conference bears testimony to our desire to bend our wills to His. However we may justify the beginnings of disunion, we lament its continuance and henceforth must labour, in penitence and faith, to build up our broken walls. . . .

More than half the world is waiting for the Gospel. At home and abroad sad multitudes are turning away in bewilderment from the Church because of its corporate feebleness. Our missions count that as a necessity which we are inclined to look on as a luxury. . . . We of the Churches represented in this Conference cannot allow our spiritual children to outpace us. We with them must gird ourselves to the task, the early beginnings of which God has so richly blessed, and labour side by side, until our common goal is reached.[9]

In nineteen days the Conference had briefly considered a vast range of subjects—the gospel, the nature of the church, the ministry, the sacraments, and so forth. It was clear that in many cases the surface had hardly been scratched and that an enormous amount of careful theological work would have to be done, if for no other purpose than to explain the churches to one

[9] *Faith and Order* (ed. H. N. Bate), p. 401.

another and to help them to see where agreements and differences really lay. So this Conference, like the others, appointed a continuation committee, charged among other things with the fairly comprehensive task of taking "whatever steps it may think wise and necessary, within the purpose of the Conference on Faith and Order, to advance the cause of Christian unity." The larger ecumenical movement was beginning to take shape. There were now in existence three continuation committees, each having in view the calling of further international Christian Conferences. And the overlap in membership was such as to indicate that it would not be possible forever to retain in three distinct compartments the interest of the churches in missions overseas, in practical Christianity, and in the Faith and Order of the Church.

To the story of the first great Conference on Faith and Order a brief postscript remains to be added. In 1929 Bishop Brent, who had in 1918 become bishop of Western New York, was once more travelling in Europe. For a long time his health had been uncertain, and he knew well that death might come to him at any time. On the way to the Mediterranean, where a cruise had been arranged for him by an admiring friend, he had reached Lausanne, the scene of his greatest effort and his greatest triumph. There on the morning of March 27 he died peacefully. According to his own wish, he was buried in the city where he died. A simple tablet on the walls of the English church in Lausanne serves to remind worshippers of one who saw more clearly than most the bright vision of the City of God, and had long dwelt in it by faith before he was called to share in the heavenly citizenship. And so we end this chapter with words of prayer written by the one who had been the inspiration of the first World Conference on Faith and Order:

O God, who hast folded back the black mantle of the night to clothe us in the golden glory of the day, chase from our hearts all gloomy thoughts and make us glad with the brightness of hope, that we may effectively aspire to unwon virtues: through Jesus Christ our Lord.

Lord Jesus, whose will it is to fold thy flock and to make us all one in thee, behold our earnestness to be gathered into the peace and unity of thy appointment. Guide us who have lost our way into the path leading to thee and to thy purpose. Enable us each and all to find thee, and in thee to find one another. Bless our efforts to follow thy counsels and in love to reason together concerning the things that separate, to the end that, misunderstanding and self-seeking and prejudice being dispelled, we may see clearly the blessed goal, and in passionate devotion pray and seek and knock, until we know as we are known and love as we are loved.[10]

[10] *Prayers of Bishop Brent,* pp. 3, 17. Used by permission of Forward Movement Publications and Harper and Brothers.

IV

Bishop Azariah and the Call to Church Union

YOU WOULD HAVE TO HAVE A VERY LARGE-SCALE MAP OF India in order to find Vellalanvilai. There is not much to distinguish this village of a thousand inhabitants from a hundred others like it, built upon the sandy soil of the *teri*[1] and shadowed by their tall and graceful palms. Yet there is one difference. All the people of Vellalanvilai are Christians; the center of the life of the village is the century-old church. And in this remote and unlikely place was born one of the greatest Christians of our own or any other age.

Vellalanvilai is about fifty miles from Cape Comorin, the southern tip of India, and so not far from the center of the first mass movement to take place in Protestant missionary history. In 1795 and 1796, in circumstances that still remain mysterious, the Lutheran missionaries baptized more than five thousand people in this area. For nearly twenty years this new and struggling church was left almost without missionary oversight, to its disadvantage in some ways and its profit in others. In many matters it was able to develop its own way of doing things and to take on from the start the lineaments of a genuinely Indian church. Later it became very strictly Anglican, with an almost exaggerated reverence for the Book of Common Prayer. Yet, for all that, living in the Tinnevelly Church was as different as could be imagined from living in the Church of England.

Almost all these first converts were drawn from the group called the Shanars, or more politely, and as they prefer to call themselves, the Nadars. Many of these people earn their living

[1] *Teri,* the sandhills rising to 200 feet in height, which fringe this part of the coast of India.

by climbing the tall palmyra tree to tap it for the sweet juice, which rises during five or six months of the year. This liquid ferments rapidly and produces a sweet and heady beer, but it can be boiled down into a coarse sugar, which was and is the main form of sweetening used throughout South India. Many of the Nadars have a little land and cattle. Long hours of hard physical work have produced among them a magnificent physique. At their first entry into history they were found sunk in deep ignorance and almost wholly illiterate; under the influence of the gospel and education they have given evidence of great gifts and have produced men and women eminent in every walk of life—bishops, cabinet ministers, doctors, teachers, and the rest.

In 1838 a Welsh missionary named John Thomas was sent to this area to guide the growing movement. He was a man of strong will and commanding energy. Seeing the Christian movement rapidly growing, he felt that it would be good to have a fine central church that would give to the scattered Christians the sense of strength and of stability. He knew nothing about architecture. However, he bought a book, and ere long there rose from the red soil the lovely church of St. Paul, built to seat 1,500 people (crossed-legged on the floor—we do not have the unnecessary luxury of pews in Tinnevelly). Then he thought it would be nice to have a spire. So he built a spire 192 feet high. The simple local people, never having seen anything of the kind before, supposed that the spire had been constructed lying flat on the ground and wondered by what witchcraft it had been raised to an upright position. Then Thomas thought it would be nice to have a bell. The bell was ordered from England, but when it arrived it was cracked. Thomas knew nothing about bell casting. However, he bought a book, dug a large hole in the ground, and recast the bell. It still chimes, though after a century the purity of its note is not quite what it was.

But Thomas rendered a far greater service to the church than any of these. He fought out the battle of the village ministry. In 1845 there were nineteen ordained ministers in Tinnevelly; eighteen of them were white and only one was Indian. It had been taken for granted that the Indian minister must learn Greek and Hebrew and do all the things that his missionary friend had done. Thomas affirmed that with a rapidly growing village church, the right course was to take the ablest of the village catechists, give them a thorough but simple course in their own language, and ordain them to the ministry. There was much opposition, but in the end Thomas had his way. The first ordination, of six candidates, took place in 1849; these men were such a success that the voice of criticism was stilled, and the Indian village ministry was established. In 1867, in the greatest ordination yet held in India, one of the candidates admitted to the ministry was a village catechist named Thomas Vedanayakam.

This good man knew little or no English. But he was a true and faithful shepherd to his flock in Vellalanvilai. In his home the Bible was law, and everything was guided by a simple and austere Christian devotion. Here, in 1874, after many years of childless marriage his wife was gladdened by the gift of a son, who was baptized by the name of Samuel Azariah, and from the moment of his birth was dedicated to the service of the Lord. It was part of the greatness of Azariah that when he was one of the most famous Christians in the world, he was still at heart a simple village boy, and that he admitted frankly on all occasions that under God he owed everything that was best in himself to the teaching and example of his mother.

It is a far cry from the palmyras and buffaloes of Vellalanvilai to the Lambeth Conference of Anglican bishops and Buckingham Palace. We must pass in silence over many stages in this great career. But three friends left such a deep mark on Azariah's character and outlook that they must be named. Like many other promising young men of that time, Azariah found his first outlet for Christian service not in the church itself but in the Y.M.C.A. There he was brought into contact with a young American, Sherwood Eddy. Eddy has had a great career of his own. But among all the good things he has done, nothing can outshine the service he rendered by showing Azariah that equal friendship between East and West is possible, by giving him confidence in himself, and by encouraging him to think out all problems for himself without depending on the judgment or verdict of others. Henry Whitehead, bishop of Madras (and brother of the famous philosopher), and his exceedingly able wife Isabel were early drawn to Azariah. They too encouraged him to read and think. Exceptional people themselves, they were perhaps the first to discern the exceptional quality of Azariah and to see that they had in their hands a possible bishop of the church.

But the decisive turning point in Azariah's career, as in that of Augustine, came from the almost fortuitous word of an unknown student. Like other Indian leaders, Azariah had been concerned that whereas missionaries from the West had been spreading the gospel all over India, Indians were doing so little for the evangelization of the non-Christian parts of their own country. With others he had founded in 1903 the Indian Missionary Society of Tinnevelly to work in the backward territories of the Nizam northwest of Madras. In his travels on behalf of the Y.M.C.A. he frequently urged Indian students with eloquence and passion to give their lives to the work of preaching the gospel to their own people. At the close of one meeting at which he had spoken, a student said to Azariah, "Why do you not go yourself?" To such a challenge there could be but one answer. The prominent Y.M.C.A. secretary became the lonely missionary. Azariah sought ordination and took up work in what was then the remote and tiger-haunted area of Dornakal. Within four years he had been chosen and consecrated as the first Indian bishop of the Anglican Church in India, in fact the first Indian bishop of any church outside Travancore, where the very ancient church of the Thomas Christians has existed from the earliest times.

By some this step forward was welcomed with enthusiasm, but not by all. Some faithful missionaries felt that the time had not yet come when an Indian could effectively exercise this great office in the church. Indian Christians of higher caste were inclined to look down their noses at this upstart who had climbed up on the shoulders of European friends. Azariah knew all this, and deeply sensitive under his confident exterior, he suffered deeply. But he held on. Within a few years he had become known as a wise and firm administrator, as a great teacher, and a loving shepherd of the flock. In the thirty years of his episcopate the Christians in his diocese grew from 50,000 to 150,000.

The secret of Azariah's life was that he lived on his knees. Like most godly Indian Christians, he was up by 4:30 every morning. At least an hour was given to prayer. He prayed every day by name for everyone who held important office in his diocese; this must have meant at least fifty names, apart from many other claims and intercessions. He was never a first-rate scholar, but he was a tireless student. The long and tedious train journeys over that extensive land would find him unaware of his surroundings and sunk in the latest English commentary on some New Testament book. The fruits of his studies were seen in the steady stream of books that came from his pen; his little book on *Christian Giving,* republished in World Christian Books, has now been translated into more than thirty languages.

We must now turn aside from Azariah's Indian ministry to his world-wide service as the apostle of Christian unity. We have already met him at the Edinburgh Conference and have heard his earnest plea for better relationships between Indian and Western servants of the Lord. From now on we shall find him at almost every important Christian gathering in the world, speaking always in terms of a sober realism that hardly hides the passionate earnestness beneath.

At Lausanne 1927 the Bishop of Dornakal was chosen to lay before the Conference the pitiful spectacle presented by the divided Christian enterprise in non-Christian lands:

"I am a Baptist," said an Indian friend to me, "not because of theology, but because of geography." Having accidentally become attached to a Church, Indian Christians do not find it difficult, when necessary, to change their ecclesiastical allegiance to a Church other than their own. . . . The feeling of very many Indian Christians is that they were not responsible for the divisions of Christendom, neither would they perpetuate them. Force of habit, financial dependence, denominational training and, above all, loyalty to their spiritual fathers, now keep them in denominational connections. But these circumstances cannot keep them apart for ever. . . . Fathers and brothers! Be patient with us if we cannot very whole-heartedly enter into the controversies of either the sixth or the sixteenth centuries. Recollection of these embitters church life; they may alienate the young Churches from all ecclesiastical connections. Unity may be theoretically a desirable ideal in Europe and America, but it is vital to the life of the Church in the mission field. The divisions of Christendom may be a source of weakness in Christian countries, but in non-Christian lands they are a sin and a scandal.[2]

Azariah's Chinese colleague, Timothy Tingfang Lew, made an even more striking conclusion to his allocution:

> To achieve unity we must follow the Saviour all the way to Golgotha, and there nail on the Cross all our personal preferences, individual habits, group prejudices, petty jealousies and deeply entrenched interests. To achieve unity we must die with Him and rise again.[3]

Ten years later, at Edinburgh 1937, we find that once again it is Azariah who is chosen to plead the cause of visible union. Do we detect in his words a certain feeling of frustration that, with all this beautiful talk about the blessings of unity, so little had happened in ten years?

> A leader of the Depressed Class in India said to me that his people had decided to give up Hinduism and were considering what religion they should accept as likely to give them a fuller and higher life. "When Christianity is mentioned," he said, "they remind me of the many divisions within the Christian Church. We are united in Hinduism, say they, and we shall become divided in Christianity. And, Sir," he said, "I had no answer to give." And need I say I had no answer to give either? . . .
>
> We wonder if you have sufficiently contemplated the grievous sin of perpetuating your divisions and your denominational bitterness in all these your daughter churches through the world. We pray that those who have risen up from the younger churches and labour for union may not be considered ill-advised and hasty, lacking in theological perception and historical perspective. We want you to take us seriously when we say that the problem of union is one of life and death with us. Do not—we plead with you—do not give us your aid to keep us separate, but lead us to union.[4]

[2] *Faith and Order* (ed. H. N. Bate), pp. 493, 495.
[3] *Faith and Order* (ed. H. N. Bate), p. 499.
[4] *The Second World Conference on Faith and Order, Edinburgh 1937* (ed. Hugh Martin, London: S.C.M. Press, 1938), pp. 53, 55.

These concluding words glance at the baleful part that the older churches with their financial dictatorship can play, consciously or unconsciously, in making permanent the divisions that the West has carried into its missionary work into the East. The same note was heard in the following year at the Tambaram Missionary Conference, in the declaration of the representatives of the younger churches:

Loyalty . . . will forbid the younger churches going forward to consummate any union unless it receives the whole-hearted support and blessing of those through whom these Churches have been planted. We are thus often torn between loyalty to our Mother Churches and loyalty to our ideal of union. We, therefore, appeal with all the fervour we possess, to the missionary societies and boards and the responsible authorities of the older Churches, to take this matter seriously to heart, to labour with the Churches in the mission field to achieve this union, to support and encourage us in all our efforts to put an end to the scandalous effects of our divisions, and to lead us in the path of union.[5]

We have detected a note of frustration and disillusionment in the utterances of some of these great leaders of the younger churches. So much less had happened than they had hoped for. Yet even at their most pessimistic they would not have said that nothing had happened. For great things had been happening outside the sphere to which so far we have directed our attention.

The little port of Tranquebar on the southeast coast of India, once a Danish settlement, is one of the holy places of the earth. There in July, 1706 the first two Protestant missionaries to Asia landed from the inhospitable ocean to find an equally inhospitable land. There just two hundred and fifty years later Rajah Manickam, tried friend of all ecumenical effort, was consecrated as the first Indian bishop of the Lutheran Churches in India. And there in 1919 a group of about thirty ministers, all of them Indians except for two foreigners, met to consider the problem of the preaching of the gospel in India. From evangelism they found themselves led on to the problem of church unity, and in

[5] *Tambaram Madras Series* (London: Oxford University Press and Edinburgh House Press, 1939), IV, 403.

the Tranquebar Manifesto they sent out a moving and effective challenge. Here are the oft-quoted words:

We believe that the union is the will of God, even as our Lord prayed that we might all be one, that the world might believe. . . . We face together the titanic task of the winning of India for Christ—one fifth of the human race. Yet, confronted by such an overwhelming responsibility, we find ourselves rendered weak and relatively impotent by our unhappy divisions—divisions for which we were not responsible, and which have been, as it were, imposed upon us from without; divisions which we did not create, and which we do not desire to perpetuate.[6]

No one knows exactly how the Manifesto was composed. Most ecumenical documents are the work of many hands, the result of endless revisions which make the JEDP of the Pentateuch seem a miracle of simplicity in comparison. Yet those who have pondered the specimens of Azariah's style quoted above are likely to think that it was his hand that drafted these crucial sentences —brief, concentrated, picturesque, decisive. Those present at the Conference believed that they had done a historic thing. Others were quick to see the prophetic significance of this challenge. Almost at once Henry Whitehead of Madras wrote:

May we not see . . . in this statement that has been issued by the pastors at Tranquebar a small cloud, no bigger it may be than a man's hand, which is destined rapidly to spread over India and descend in showers of blessing over the whole Christian Church?

For this was not just another general panegyric of unity, as something that ought to come into being but unfortunately does not. It was a direct and deliberate challenge to action. The Faith and Order movement, with an almost exaggerated conscientiousness, has kept itself strictly within the limits of theory. It has been an affair of theologians, scrutinizing and debating doctrines and definitions. Whenever anyone has gone beyond this and temerariously attempted to formulate a plan by

[6] This historic document is cited in full in Bengt Sundkler, *The Church of South India* (London: Lutterworth Press, 1954), p. 101.

which divided churches might be united, Faith and Order has indicated that such lower and concrete concerns are in no sense its affair. It may chronicle them; it refrains from judging and leaves judgment entirely to the churches which are the responsible bodies. But the men of Tranquebar had not talked about *union;* they were thinking in terms of *the union,* an actual union to be brought about between the Anglican Church in South India and that earlier amalgam (1908) of Congregational, Presbyterian, and other interests which was known as the South India United Church.

Official negotiations were set on foot. An invitation was issued to all the other churches to join in. Only the British Methodists responded. And so the Joint Committee on Church Union in South India was formed and began its work. Twenty-eight years were to pass before hope passed into thanksgiving, with the inauguration of the Church of South India in September, 1947. And indeed the task set before the committee was hard enough. Here on the one side were staunch Anglo-Catholics, determined not to jeopardize one particle of the sacramental and historical theology of their church. On another side were rigid English Independents, who entered into the negotiations convinced that episcopacy could not mean anything but ecclesiastical tyranny. The Basel Mission brought in a continental group, which did not know the English language well and which was wholly unfamiliar with English theology and ways of thinking. Nationally and ecclesiastically, it was a remarkable cross section of the Christian churches that met year after year in this fantastic, and as it often seemed desperate, search for Christian union.

A great mythology has grown up round the South India negotiations. Those who took part in it have been represented alternatively as old men in a hurry and young men in a hurry, as nice but rather ignorant people—two of whom happened to have obtained a triple first class at the University of Cambridge, as earnest pastors who were determined to force union through regardless of any theological issues that might come up. In point of fact they were a patient, rather learned, very human group of Christians, who believed themselves to have heard a call from God, and were prepared to sit down year after year to listen to the voice of God. They saw the immense practical advantages which would follow upon union, but this was not the consideration that had led them into the enterprise and kept them working through a whole generation of human life. They held on simply because they believed union to be the will of God, and because they had come to believe that to abandon these discussions would be treachery to the name of Christ. Every point of theology as of practice was patiently discussed. Every suggestion, from whatever quarter received, was weighed with discrimination and unhurried judgment. The delegates remained in close touch with the authorities of their own churches in India and elsewhere and with the best theological authorities in the whole of Christendom. An enormous correspondence developed.

Professor Sunkler has written 457 pages on this exciting chapter of church history; and even in this classic work of scholarly research the half has not been told. Those who loved through those years ("lived" is what I meant, but "loved" is what my typewriter wrote, and perhaps the typewriter judged better than I; we did come to love one another in those years) can look back on countless moments of frustration and almost despair and on some moments of illumination, when God seemed to show a way through what had appeared to be an impassable jungle. And so at last it was done. Line by line and clause by clause the Scheme of Union was forged. The churches accepted it. The stage was set for the glorious act of union.

But here once again we touch the pathos and the tragedy of ecumenical work. The diocese of Dornakal had voted unanimously in favor of the Scheme of Union. And then just a month before the whole Anglican Church in India was due to record its final vote, the great bishop died, full of years and honor, worn out with the care of all the churches and with the pastoral labors to which he had given himself unstintingly almost till the last day of his life. He had labored; other men were to enter into his labors.

The Church of South India now has twelve years of history behind it. It has been widely recognized as the greatest venture yet made anywhere in the direction of church union. What has come of it all?

It has become clear that the act of union did not immediately and of itself release a great new flood of spiritual power. The unity of the church and its renewal are both good things, but we must not suppose that one will necessarily lead to the other. Each must be sought independently and for its own sake. Yet the new church has stood, in the face of much criticism and some disapproval. Those who live in it and for it find it an immense advantage that the old Western names—Anglican, Methodist, and so on—have just disappeared; this is the Church of South India and nothing else. This is no foreign body, no colony of the Western powers. It is an Indian Church, fully self-governing, dependent on no one outside itself, with its roots in the soil of India or rather with roots only in Christ, who died for India no less than for the rest of the world.

One feature of the organization of the church has come in for the harshest criticism. It was agreed that a period of thirty years should be allowed for growing together and for the accomplishment of the union. No one would be ordained or reordained. All ministers of all the churches would enter on an equality. Steps would be taken to safeguard for every congregation the kind of ministry to which it was accustomed. But all would equally share in the government of the church, and all ministers would be equally eligible for appointment to the episcopate. This plan caused considerable difficulties in the relationships of the new church with the Anglican churches. And yet through the successive stages of the Lambeth Conferences of 1948 and 1958, the English Convocations of 1950 and 1955, and the General Convention of the Episcopal Church of America in 1958 hard attitudes have softened, and a general acceptance has taken the place of a tendency towards rejection. The Archbishop of Canterbury made history in 1958 when he invited two South India bishops, one formerly a Methodist, the other formerly a Presbyterian, to take part in the consecration of a bishop of the Church of England.

South India has rightly attracted more attention than any other plan of union. But it is far from standing alone in the countries of the younger churches.

The Church of Christ in China came into existence in 1927 on the basis of a very simple "Bond of Union." It brought together a wide range of churches—no Lutherans and no Anglicans—in a real fellowship but with so much independence for each church that this might seem to be rather a federation than a genuinely united church.

In Japan during World War II, under pressure from the government almost all the Protestant bodies were merged in the Church of Christ in Japan, the Nippon Kirisuto Kyodan. As soon as the war was over and pressure was relaxed, a good many of these bodies resumed their independence. Yet most of the Presbyterians, Methodists, and Congregationalists remained in the Kyodan, which is today the largest Christian body in Japan. It has recently put out its confession of faith and has manifested its determination to take its stand as one of the historic churches of the Christian world.

In the Philippines, as in Japan, government pressure during the war forced on union. Later a series of kaleidoscopic changes dissolved some unions and created others. But since 1948 the United Church of Christ in the Philippines seems to have settled down to a stable and orderly existence. The Philippines are unlike any other country in the world. For four centuries the mass of the population has been at least nominally Roman Catholic. There is now no background of any great non-Christian culture. The Filipino Christian is quite content to be a Christian and nothing else and is not at all worried if being a Christian involves some borrowing from the West. Vigorously independent in outlook, he is quite prepared to take on any challenge from the Westerner and to stand on his own feet. It is perhaps no accident that Bishop Sobrepena of the United Church was president of the East Asia Christian Conferences held at Prapat in 1957 and at Kuala Lumpur in 1959.

So in four great countries of Asia we see already united churches in which a variety of traditions have been successfully brought together. And this is not the end of the story. Ceylon and North India have before them complete schemes of union. In these an ingenious attempt has been made to eliminate the "interim period" of South India through a commissioning ceremony, by which at the inauguration of union all ministers of all the uniting churches may be brought together into one common ministry. The churches have not yet finally voted on these schemes, but there is considerable probability that they will be adopted in the near future.

The influence of South India has spilled over into Africa. Nigeria has come forward with a scheme which very closely resembles that of South India, including the interim period. The latest news is that the movement in favor of unity is gaining in strength. This country of more than thirty million people will become politically independent in 1961; it is the feeling of many Christians that the churches should show the state the way and should be the first to find their unity and their independence.

In the meantime what has been happening in the West? Have the older churches made up their minds to turn their backs on the things that divide and to seek and ensue a genuine unity in Christ? There is much talk of unity, many negotiations. But it seems that the resolution to act is lacking. It is possible to make many excuses for the older churches. Traditions are longer and more deeply ingrained. Vested interests are strong and complex —and so on and so on. But perhaps the problem was stated quite succinctly and definitively by Timothy Lew as long ago as 1927. The Western churches are not one, because they are not willing to follow their Savior all the way to Golgotha. We still need the leaders of the younger churches to issue the challenge and to issue it in such rousing and irresistible tones that even the dead must awake and give ear.

V

Archbishop Germanos and the Orthodox

In A.D. 668 the Pope sent Theodore of Tarsus to England to be Archbishop of Canterbury. The aged compatriot of Paul, already sixty-six years old, set out without hesitation for the distant, barbarous, and scarcely known island on the very fringe of the Christian world. In the twenty-two years during which he served that young and so far rather shapeless church, he left a deeper impression upon it than any of his successors in the see of Canterbury. The twenty-nine years' residence of Germanos Strenopoulos in London as Metropolitan of Thyateira, Exarch of the West, and personal representative of the Ecumenical Patriarch of Constantinople in the countries of western Europe did not perhaps produce such visible and notable effects. Yet it contributed in no small measure to the participation of the ancient Orthodox churches in the ecumenical movement. A powerful factor in this development was the confidence which Germanos inspired both among his fellow Orthodox and in the churches of the West.

The Church of England had had a variety of contacts, almost always friendly, with the Orthodox churches of the East. In the seventeenth century a number of distinguished chaplains of the Levant Company had lived in Orthodox lands and written a series of remarkable books. In the reign of William III there had been the fantastic plan for a church of the Greek nation in London; it being understood that in a church built under the patronage of the Church of England as by law established there were to be no *ikons* or other signs of idolatrous worship! It is hardly surprising that this scheme came to nothing. In 1896 an Anglican bishop, the great Mandell Creighton of London, had journeyed to Moscow for the coronation of the Emperor and had been somewhat perturbed to find that he was expected to wear a magnificent cope, lent by Westminster Abbey, while eating his dinner. But no Orthodox had been present at the Edinburgh Conference of 1910, and as the modern ecumenical movement began to take shape, it was by no means certain that the Orthodox churches would wish to have anything to do with it.

That ecumenical veteran Adolph Keller has left us a vivid picture of the surprise, almost consternation, of a group of church leaders, met to make the preliminary plans for the Stockholm Conference, when the Orthodox churches literally burst in upon them in the persons of three archbishops, bearded and swathed in the flowing black robes that are worn by prelates of those churches. It was in 1920 that this group met in Geneva, under the presidency of Archbishop Soederblom. Delegates were eyeing one another somewhat uncomfortably and uncertainly, since the terrible question of "war-guilt" was high in the minds of many, and relations between the Germans and the delegates of other countries were strained, if not positively hostile. It was at this moment that Archbishop Germanos, at that time Metropolitan of Seleucia, entered with his two companions, charged by the Ecumenical Patriarchate to carry a message of good will, and a letter of the utmost importance, to this first international Christian gathering after the first war. The Archbishop read his letter in Greek. The assembled brethren were duly impressed at being addressed in the accents, more or less, of Paul, but could make nothing of Greek pronounced in the modern fashion of Constantinople. Fortunately, Soederblom, who always seemed to be able to do the right thing at the right moment, produced out of his entourage a Swedish pastor who could speak modern Greek, and the curse of Babel was removed from the assembly.

But we must go back a little in our history. Germanos had been born in 1872, a Turkish subject, in a small village in Thrace. But he was Greek by race and speech and feeling. He went to study for the priesthood at the Orthodox seminary of Halki, a small island in the Sea of Marmora, where Orthodox students for the priesthood still receive their training. After a period of study in Germany, in which he gave evidence of brilliant intellectual gifts, Germanos was called back to his old student home as teacher. After a few years as lecturer he was appointed at the early age of thirty five to the high office of rector of the seminary. For fifteen years he remained in this quiet spot, reading widely, thinking, praying, pondering the nature of the church, impressing on his students his own deep and simple piety. After some years he was raised to the episcopate with the title of Metropolitan of Seleucia, but he remained at Halki and carried on with his quiet work as lecturer. But increasingly he had become the trusted confidant and adviser of the Patriarch and of others who were concerned about the wider life of the Orthodox churches and their relationships with the rest of the Christian world.

The letter which Germanos carried from the patriarchate of Constantinople to the church leaders assembled in Geneva was one of the most notable documents in the whole history of interchurch relationships. This was the period of new hope that had dawned upon the world with the formation of the League of Nations, hope soon to be dashed to the ground by the failure of America to enter the League and by the failure of the League itself to act with the probity and courage which alone could have established it as a force for righteousness and peace among the nations. Later in the same year the Lambeth Conference of Anglican bishops was to issue another notable document, its "appeal to all Christian people" in favor of Christian unity. But to the astonishment of all those who supposed that the Orthodox churches were still living in the Middle Ages and were unaware of anything that was happening in the modern world, the ancient Church of Constantinople took the lead and suddenly came forward with proposals that gave evidence of breadth of outlook and of an astonishingly tolerant spirit. No one knows who wrote the "Encyclical letter from the Patriarchate of Constantinople, Unto all the Churches of Christ wheresoever they be." In January, 1920 the patriarchal throne was vacant, and its affairs were under the direction of a locum tenens. It is believed, however, that though the voice was the voice of the church, the hand and the pen were those of Germanos, who thus rendered his first outstanding service to the cause of better understanding between the great churches of the world.

It is clear that those who sent out the document were deeply under the influence of the ideals of the League of Nations. They would regard it as lamentable if the churches were to "fall piteously behind the political authorities, who, truly applying the spirit of the Gospel and of the Justice of Christ, have under happy auspices already instituted the League of Nations, for the defence of right and the cultivation of love and harmony among the nations." But the document is a genuinely Christian appeal and not a political manifesto. It opens with ringing words:

> Our Church is of the opinion that a closer intercourse with each other and a mutual understanding between the several Christian Churches is not prevented by the doctrinal differences existing between them, and that such an understanding is highly desirable and necessary, and in many ways useful in the well-conceived interest of each one of the Churches taken apart and as a whole Christian body, as also for preparing and facilitating the complete and blessed union which may some day be attained with God's help.[1]

It goes on to suggest no less than twelve methods by which the churches could help one another forwards in the path of better understanding and closer union. Among these are (d) by an intercourse between theological schools and the representatives of theological science . . . , (e) by the exchange of students between the seminaries of the different Churches, (f) by convening pan-Christian conferences to examine questions of common interest to all Churches.[2]

It seemed that a similar spirit of hope and desire for union was blowing simultaneously in all the churches.

Two years later in 1922 Archbishop Germanos was sent to London, with the new title of Metropolitan of Thyateira, to supervise all the Greek-speaking congregations in the West of Europe. His many travels soon made him a familiar figure in all the countries of Western Europe. In some ways his appointment had come too late. He never learned to speak English fluently and did not take much part in public life in England. But he was always there. We shall find him at almost every large international gathering of Christians, from Stockholm 1925

[1] The full text of the document is in G. K. A. Bell, *Documents on Christian Unity,* first series (London: Oxford University Press, 1924), p. 44-48.

[2] *Op. cit.,* p. 46.

onwards. Always his influence was exercised in favor of charity and larger mutual understanding. Far ahead of almost all other Orthodox prelates in his knowledge and understanding of churches outside the Orthodox world, he managed to combine a firm, though always courteous, insistence on Orthodox principles, with a deep and eager desire for inward and outward unity among all those who profess the faith of Christ.

It must not be thought that Germanos stood alone. With him were such outstanding figures as Hamilcar Alivisatos of the University of Athens, Bishop Cassian of the Russian Church in exile in Paris, and Bishop Nicolai of Ochrida in Serbia. Through the efforts of these men and of others like them Orthodox participation in the ecumenical movement has been a great reality. Yet there has always been present a certain factor of anxiety, and the Protestant churches have never been able to feel quite sure that they could count on their Orthodox brethren as being fully committed to the ecumenical cause. We have already taken note of the Orthodox protest at Lausanne 1927 (it is said that Archbishop Germanos, having read it, returned to his seat, his face streaming with tears). We shall find that at almost every similar gathering the Orthodox have found it necessary to make a separate statement, and in one way or another to safeguard themselves against any misunderstanding of their position.

A number of reasons may be put forward as accounting for this element of uncertainty in Orthodox ecumenical activity.

There is, first of all, the Orthodox understanding of the church and its nature. In the eyes of all Orthodox Christians, the Orthodox churches together make up the church—there is no other. In the fifth century the Far Eastern churches lapsed into heresy. Between the seventh and the eleventh centuries the Roman Church became at least schismatic; whereas in the Nicene Creed the Orthodox churches proclaim that the Holy Spirit proceeds from the Father, the Roman Church has added the fatal words "and from the Son," *filioque*. Even if this addition is not intended to convey any heretical meaning, a local church like the Church of Rome has no business to make a change in a creed which is the expression of the faith of the whole church. Protestant bodies are voluntary societies of pious laymen, with no guaranteed ministry, grace, or sacraments. (A partial exception is made in favor of the Anglican and Old Catholic churches.) Some Orthodox churches carry out their principles in such logical and ruthless fashion that a Christian who passes from some other church to the Orthodox is rebaptized, though such repetition is condemned as blasphemy by the vast majority of Christian churches. The Orthodox have the proud sense that they alone have maintained the purity of the faith. Western Christianity may represent the teaching of Paul; the Orthodox churches alone have understood the fulness of truth as it is set forth in the Gospel and Epistles of John.

From this understanding of the nature of the church certain corollaries with regard to Christian unity naturally follow. All that the other churches have to do is to return to the unity that they have forsaken, and so the oneness of all Christ's people, which is already visible in the Orthodox churches, will be restored. If Orthodox go to international Christian assemblies, they do not go to learn—they have nothing to learn; they go to testify to the truth which they alone possess in its fulness. Other Christians in the ecumenical movement may not agree with these claims of the Orthodox; it is most important that they should understand that this is what the Orthodox really believe, and that in any honest movement for Christian unity they, like other Christians, must be given the fullest freedom for the expression of their convictions. They cannot be expected to subscribe to any statement which seems to them to impair the full and majestic completeness of their claims.

The Orthodox are hampered and perplexed by their own lack of unity.

We must not forget that not all the churches which call themselves "Orthodox" are recognised as such by the Orthodox churches of Greece and Russia. There is the group of Far Eastern churches to which we have already alluded. These include the Armenians, the Copts in Egypt, the Church of Ethiopia, and the very ancient "Syrian" Church in South India. All these adhere to the ecumenical movement. There are happy signs today of better relations between them and the Orthodox churches, but there is no intercommunion; here we enter a world even older and remoter from our Western ways of thinking than that of the Orthodox churches of the nearer East.

Officially, the head of the Orthodox churches is the Ecumenical Patriarch at Constantinople. But many circumstances combine to prevent him from exercising an effective headship, such as that which the Pope exercises over the Church of Rome. For long centuries Christians were oppressed and harried by their Turkish masters. Patriarchs were assassinated, exiled, or replaced at the whim of the Sultan. Even now the Patriarch exercises direct jurisdiction only over a very small number of Orthodox Christians resident in Turkey and in certain regions of northern Greece.

With the coming of the independence of the modern nations, each regional church has claimed to be autonomous and autocephalous, with its own patriarch, though standing in a relationship of loyalty and affection to Constantinople. This has resulted in a large number of independent jurisdictions, generally linked to the use of a local language. Almost all these jurisdictions have been reproduced in America by those who have come from the various countries, to the confusion of those who try to understand the situation of the Orthodox in the United States.

There is a considerable psychological difference as between Orthodox who speak Greek and regard themselves as the direct heirs of the great Greek Fathers—Athanasius, Chrysostom, and the rest—those who speak Arabic, and those who speak one of the Slavonic languages.

There is a sharp and unhealed division between various groups of Russian origin. A few hundred yards from the room in Geneva in which I am writing is a beautiful Russian church. This belongs to what is known as the Karlovtsy group—the conservative element, which has utterly rejected the Russian revolution and is regarded as heretical by the Church of Moscow today. A large section of the Russian emigration in France has put itself under Constantinople, an action bitterly resented by the Patriarch of Moscow. Then there are those, in western Europe as in Russia itself, who have accepted the revolution and are in possession of passports issued by the present Russian government.

There is fierce rivalry between the Patriarchates of Constantinople and Moscow. Who is the real head of the Orthodox Churches? Historically, Constantinople has the better claim. But Moscow has an answer. In 1594 Moscow was raised to the status of an independent patriarchate. This was providentially ordered. The first Rome had fallen into heresy. The second Rome, Byzantium, the city of Constantine, had fallen under the domination of the infidel Turk. Now God had raised up Moscow, the third Rome, to be the light of the world, so that from holy Russia the gospel might come back both to the paganized West and to the countries once Christian in which the Muslim now proudly rules. It may seem strange to us that the Patriarch of Moscow should seriously take this view of his own position and should claim to be the divinely appointed head of all the Christians in the world. There is no doubt whatever that this is his view—and to be ecumenical means to take seriously all the views held by other Christians, however strange or bizarre they may seem to us.

In 1948 the Patriarch of Moscow convened in Moscow a conference of heads and representatives of Autocephalous Orthodox Churches. Constantinople emphatically denied the right of Moscow to call any general Orthodox conference. Inevitably, Germanos was present, to partake in a friendly manner in the celebrations of the fifth centenary of the granting of autocephalous status to the Church of Russia. But he did not sign any of the resolutions of the Conference, and gave no sign of recognizing that it had any authoritative status in the Orthodox world.

These different groups of Orthodox have taken up remarkably different attitudes towards the ecumenical movement and the World Council of Churches. On the whole the churches of Greek and Arabic speech and the Russians in exile have warmly participated. Russia and the other churches of Slavonic speech under communist domination have taken up a much more cautous, critical, and sometimes even hostile attitude.

The Moscow Conference of 1948 discussed the question of the participation of the Slavonic churches in the World Council of Churches and passed a quite astonishing series of resolutions. A few extracts may be given:

a) The aims of the ecumenical movement . . . do not correspond to the ideal of Christianity or the aims of the Church of Christ, as understood by the Orthodox Church.

b) The directing of their efforts into the main stream of social and political life, and to the creating of an "Ecumenical Church" as an important international power, appear to be as it were a falling into that temptation which was rejected by Christ in the desert, and a turning of the Church on to the path of attempting to catch human souls in the nets of Christ by un-Christian methods.

d) The theme of the reunion of the Churches on dogmatic and doctrinal grounds . . . is no longer discussed, only a secondary pedagogical significance is ascribed to it for some future generation. Thus our contemporary ecumenical movement does not safeguard the task of the reunion of the Churches by the way and means of grace.

e) The lowering of the requirements for conditions of unity to a single one, namely that of recognizing Jesus Christ as Our Lord, debases Christian doctrine to the kind of faith which according to the Apostle is available to devils.[3]

Such resolutions cannot be read without astonishment. The kindest interpretation is that no one among those responsible for the drafting was able to read any of the official languages of the ecumenical movement (English, French, and German), and that they were dependent on very imperfect translations. Even so it seems strange that the delegates should not have been aware that the basis of the Faith and Order Movement, taken up and adopted by the World Council of Churches, is the confession of faith in Jesus Christ *as God and Savior.* A resolution which lamentably misquoted and then misinterpreted so fundamental a document could hardly be taken very seriously in the rest of the Christian world.

In a statement released during the first Assembly of the World Council of Churches in 1948, the General Secretary pointed out the one hopeful element in the situation:

The reasons given for the negative decision are based upon

[3] Proceedings of the Conference of the Heads of the Autocephalous Orthodox Churches, held in Moscow, July, 1948 (E. Tr., Y. M. C. A. Press, Paris, 1952), p. 240-41.

a complete misunderstanding of the true nature of our movement—a misunderstanding such as can easily arise in a Church whose leaders have no first-hand knowledge of ecumenical life. If we succeed . . . in making it clear that so far from pursuing political purposes we have no other concern than the concern for the Lordship of Christ everywhere . . . it may yet be possible to remove the existing misunderstanding. . . . In any case our course is clear. We should keep the door open for the Church of Russia and other Orthodox Churches not already represented among us.[4]

Although by doing so we shall break the chronological order of events which we have been roughly following, it may be well here to carry forward the story of relations between the Church of Russia and the ecumenical movement.

Between 1948 and 1958 there had been considerable exchange of documents between Geneva and Moscow and also between the Church of Russia and other parts of the Christian world. For instance a delegation of Anglican theologians, under the leadership of the Archbishop of York (Ramsey), had visited Moscow in 1956. At last in 1958 the Orthodox of Moscow felt that the time had come when they could take one cautious step forward and authorize three representative churchmen from the Russian Church to meet with three representatives of the World Council of Churches.

The meetings took place quietly in Utrecht between August 7 and 9, 1958. One of the representatives of the World Council was the Metropolitan James, who for some years had been the representative of the Ecumenical Patriarch at Geneva, and is now Greek Archbishop in New York. The official communique setting forth the results of the meeting is, as is the way of such communiques, very cautious in its language. Yet it contains some momentous expressions. Both sides agreed that they "shared the concern for the unity of Christians and the manifestation of their unity in the life of the Churches." They agreed that they shared "a deep concern for world peace with justice and freedom." The Russians undertook "that they would give a

[4] Mimeographed document, quoted by permission of the General Secretary of the World Council of Churches.

report to the Patriarch and the Holy Synod of their Church and that they would do so in a spirit of full sympathy with the fundamental principles of the ecumenical movement."

Much had been gained. More was to follow in 1959. While this chapter was being written, the Central Committee of the World Council of Churches was meeting in Rhodes—the first important meeting of an ecumenical body to be held in an Orthodox country. For the first time two observers from the Church of Russia were present with the full authorization of their church. It is likely that years will yet have to pass before the Church of Russia sees its way to becoming a member church of the World Council, but at least the process of mutual education in the ecumenical setting has begun—and here, as in so many things, it is the first step that counts.[5]

With two remaining Orthodox difficulties we can deal more briefly.

It is the curious fact that in the Orthodox world, and especially in Greece, the majority of the theologians are laymen. For instance, at the University of Athens all the professors of the faculty of theology are laymen, who combine in delicate equilibrium a genuine Orthodox faith with theological insights that have come to them from other churches during periods of study abroad. Most of the bishops have been monks, and though admirable in their pastoral work, have little knowledge of the modern world and only slight acquaintance with the technical details of theology. When such prelates have attended ecumenical meetings, they have tended to feel themselves confused and isolated, understanding none of the official languages and being dependent on perhaps inadequate translations for their knowledge of what is going on. But according to Orthodox tradition, it is the hierarchy alone that should pronounce on all matters of faith and order.

This difficulty perhaps underlies the hesitating attitude of the Church of Greece towards ecumenical affairs. If the Russians complain that the World Council devotes too little time and thought to questions of faith and order, the Greeks have been

[5] Shortly before I received the galley proofs of this book in Geneva, six representatives of the World Council of Churches made a journey to Russia at the invitation of the Patriarch.

inclined to think that the ecumenical movement would do better to limit itself to purely practical questions, rather than become involved in matters of faith and order, on which it is very ill qualified to pronounce. There have even been moments at which it seemed likely that the Church of Greece would withdraw altogether from ecumenical discussions. This extreme step has been avoided, and the malaise and anxiety seen at least for the time being to have been exorcised.

Finally, we come to the vexed question of missions. To us in the West, missions are naturally interpreted as meaning the preaching of the gospel to non-Christian nations which have never heard the gospel. To the Orthodox the word has another and far more sinister connotation. For centuries they have had not merely to maintain themselves with great difficulty against Muslim aggression; they have also had to defend themselves against the attacks of fellow Christians, who have tried to take advantage of their misfortunes to subvert their ancient faith. For centuries the Roman Catholics have maintained their "missions" in Orthodox countries and have spared neither money nor effort in the attempt to draw the Orthodox away from their own allegiance and into the fold of Rome. The world has seen the discreditable spectacle of groups of Christians being forcibly converted in one direction, and then perhaps with a change of political control, being forcibly converted back in the opposite direction. But it is not only the Roman Catholics who have offended. Some Protestant churches have also maintained missions in Greece and Turkey and elsewhere. Often these have done splendid work in educating those who were to be the young leaders of the newly independent nations. But some have made no secret of their view that the old churches are so corrupt that anyone who really wishes to follow Christ must necessarily come out of them and find another way. As a result the very word "mission," with its special connotation of proselytism from one Christian body to another, has come to stink in the nostrils of the Orthodox world.

This is likely to be one of the main matters of ecumenical debate in the two years subsequent to the publication of this book. There is no easy answer.

Are we to say that in no circumstances whatever may a

Christian leave the church in which he was brought up to join another? If so, what are the Orthodox churches doing in the West and in Africa? Have they not gathered in a certain number of Christians who were Anglican or Protestant or something else? If this is not proselytism, what is it?

An acceptable solution will come only if the Orthodox churches begin again to have real missions of their own. The Russian Church did great work in gathering in the pagan tribes of Siberia. There was the famous mission of Bishop Nikolai in Japan, of which today only fragments are left. But at the moment in the whole Orthodox world there is hardly anything that could honestly be called missionary enterprise. The Church of Greece is training some students from Uganda, but it is not yet clear whether the Orthodox church in that country has any stability or whether it is merely a splinter church, temporarily separated from the larger and more stable churches of Uganda.

In this matter it is perhaps the Church of Greece that ought to give the lead. If that church, which has now had more than a century in which to gather its forces after the long centuries of Muslim oppression, would take over some area in Africa, in which no word of the gospel has ever yet been heard, and would set to work from the start to bring untouched pagan people into the church, it would learn at firsthand some of the lessons that the Protestant churches have learned over two centuries of trial and error. It would learn anew the true meaning of the word "mission." Many of the younger leaders are eager to see the church move forward into such an experiment. If this could come about, it would be perhaps the most important ecumenical advance of the middle years of the twentieth century. A church in movement discovers what the ecumenical adventure really means.

VI

William Temple and World-wide Ecumenism

In the Roman Catholic and Eastern churches bishops are not allowed to marry, but in the Anglican churches they are. So it can sometimes happen that father and son are both bishops at the same time. In 1958 Bishop Henry Sherrill ended his distinguished tenure of the office of Presiding Bishop of the Protestant Episcopal Church by presiding at the consecration of his own son Edmund as Bishop of Central Brazil. But it only rarely happens that a son succeeds to a see of which his father had earlier been bishop, and only once in history has it come about that the son of an Archbishop of Canterbury has himself been appointed as "Primate of All England."

At the end of the nineteenth century Frederick Temple, Archbishop of Canterbury, was among the greatest churchmen in the world. Gifted with a powerful mind and the capacity for lucid and forceful expression, famous for his abrupt replies to silly questions, with a rugged outward strength concealing infinite tenderness within—when Frederick Temple moved among men, they sometimes felt as though one of the old gods had come down again and was walking the earth as in the legends of classic times. The Archbishop had remained unmarried until the age of fifty-five. When he was sixty years old his second son was born and was baptized by the name William.

So William, born in the purple, grew up at Fulham Palace, the home of the Bishop of London. When he was thirteen, he moved across the Thames to Lambeth Palace, accompanying his father, who in 1895 had been appointed to the see of Canterbury. It seemed that fortune had given William Temple every good gift—the example of a wonderful father, early training in a simple, manly form of the Christian faith, a nimble mind, a cheerful disposition, and countless friends. But one thing fortune had not given—the good gift of health. In later years what most people noted in the Archbishop were his jovial, friendly disposition and his reverberating laugh. Few except his intimate friends knew that his whole life was an endless struggle with gout, one of the most painful and incapacitating of sicknesses. Undergraduates at Cambridge smiled, and so did William Temple, when the Archbishop of York, as he then was, had to be wheeled to the Senate House in a Bath chair in order to receive his honorary degree of Doctor of Divinity. It seemed hard that a lifelong teetotaler should be afflicted with a disease generaly associated with excessive indulgence in the pleasures of port wine. They could not guess, and perhaps only Mrs. Temple fully knew, the severity of the battle that the Archbishop had to fight. Very few had any idea that he could speak with such penetrating power just because he himself had so often passed through dark places, and that his wonderful spiritual power was a power born of suffering patiently endured.

In early days, however, everything seemed smiling and prosperous for the young William Temple. After a brilliant career at school and college he was elected a Fellow of Queen's College, Oxford, and settled down to study hard and to teach. Everyone predicted a brilliant future for him; he gave the impression of doing anything that he wanted to do without effort and with superb competence. A pretty picture of him in these early days has been left by Ronald (later Monsignor) Knox, himself the son of an Anglican bishop, in his poem "Absolute and Abitofhell," a marvellously skillful parody of Dryden's famous "Absalom and Achitophel." This is how Knox saw Temple:

> First, from the Public Schools—*Lernaean Bog*—
> No paltry Bulwark, stood the form of *OG*.
> A man so broad, to some he seemed to be
> Not one, but all mankind in effigy:
> Who, brisk in Term, a Whirlwind in the Long,
> Did everything by turns, and nothing wrong,
> Bill'd at each Lecture-hall from Thames to Tyne
> As Thinker, Usher, Statesman or Divine.[1]

[1] *Essays in Satire* (London: A. P. Watt & Son and Sheed & Ward Ltd).

What purpose were all these manifold gifts destined to serve? When Temple was a schoolboy, he told Eleanor MacDougall, later first principal of the Women's Christian College, Madras, that when he grew up he was going to be a missionary of the Church Missionary Society. Schoolboys often forget their earlier ideals in the excitement of making a career. Not so Temple. In 1908, when he was twenty-six, he offered to the Society and was accepted. Everything had been arranged; he was to go to India as Principal of St. John's College, Agra. Then at the last moment, to their eternal shame, the authorities of the Church of England stepped in and told Temple that he was so valuable in England that he must stay at home. I do not think that anyone who knew Temple well can doubt that, if he had been able to spend ten years in India at that formative period of his life, he would have been an even greater man than he grew to be. Firsthand contact with the problems of a non-Christian religion and the experience of life in a younger church would have enlarged and balanced that immense understanding of the problems of the West into which he gradually grew.

There followed a good many years of uncertainty and even of frustration. For a few years Temple was head master of Repton School, where he did well but not outstandingly well. Then he was rector of St. James' Church, Piccadilly, London, now in its restored form after the bombing one of the most beautiful places of worship in the Christian world. There he read widely —he claimed to be one of the few Anglicans to have read through the *Summa* of Thomas Aquinas, a formidable task—preached steadily on John's Gospel, and laid the foundations for those remarkable *Readings in St. John's Gospel,* a work of later years which has rightly been called "the greatest devotional treatise written by an English Churchman since William Law's *A Serious Call to a Devout and Holy Life.*" Leaving St. James', he gave himself to campaigning on behalf of that movement, "Life and Liberty," which, after World War I, gave to the Church of England the rudiments of the self-government which other Anglican churches much more fully enjoy. But this was not what people expected; there was a widespread feeling that there were depths in Temple that had not yet been revealed, gifts that had not yet been stirred into self-expression.

At last his day came. In 1921, at the age of thirty-nine he was appointed Bishop of Manchester. Faced by a task that was worthy of all his gifts, he grew rapidly in every way and put forth in many directions those great powers which until then had seemed so largely latent.

From early years Temple, like his father, had been deeply interested in the so-called working class. For a good many years he was a member of the Labor Party. In 1905 he had joined the Workers' Educational Association, a voluntary body which aimed at making higher education available to working men; he was president of the Association from 1908 to 1924. This meant that he was far more closely in touch than most ecclesiastics with that movement for social justice and a better ordering of society that was to find expression in the COPEC Conference and later in the international movement of Life and Work.

In these years Temple proved himself unique in his power of presenting the gospel to students in terms which they could regard as intellectually respectable, and which yet conveyed a challenge to what would now be called an existential decision. The greatest of all his university missions was that to Oxford, where spiritual life had burned rather low, in 1931. The closing scene is so striking that it must be described in full in the words of Temple's biographer, F. A. Iremonger. As the closing act of the mission, the hymn "When I Survey the Wondrous Cross" was being sung.

Before the last verse, Temple stopped the singing and said: "I want you to read over this verse before you sing it. They are tremendous words. If you mean them with all your hearts, sing them as loud as you can. If you don't mean them at all, keep silent. If you mean them even a little, and want to mean them more, sing them very softly." There was dead silence . . . and then—to hear Isaac Watt's words

> Were the whole realm of nature mine,
> That were an offering far too small;
> Love so amazing, so divine,
> Demands my soul, my life, my all

whispered by the voices of 2,000 young men and women was

(in the recollection of one of them) "an experience never to be erased from my memory until the whole tablet is blotted." [2]

During these years, in the midst of endless other preoccupations Temple found time to write a series of memorable books. As Archbishop of York (a position which he held from 1929 to 1942) he managed to produce in his spare time an impressive set of Gifford Lectures, *Nature, Man and God* (1932-4), a comprehensive survey of the Christian faith in the light of the liberal understanding of revelation, of the nature and of the destiny of man. Certainly no better book from this point of view has ever been written. The main lines of Temple's thinking had taken shape by 1921, that is to say before England began to become aware of the thought of Karl Barth. There was a close friendship between Temple and Reinhold Niebuhr, but Temple had little understanding of or sympathy for the kind of insights that are associated with the names of Barth, Niebuhr, and Paul Tillich. This means that students today, reading his works, are likely to find that, to use a metaphor, his wave length is not the same as theirs—the problems with which he is concerned are not the same as those with which they have been wrestling. Therefore, at the moment he may have little to say to them. But this is likely to be only a temporary eclipse; there is a great deal in Temple's thinking that is of permanent value, and his work, like that of his great Scottish contemporary John Oman, is likely to come back into popularity and esteem.

Here, however, we are mainly concerned with Temple's ecumenical work and with the development of the ecumenical movement during the years in which he was its most prominent figure.

As a young man Temple had been present at the Edinburgh Conference of 1910, one of that remarkable group of promising young men who had been brought together by J. H. Oldham to serve as ushers at the Conference. But his first direct participation in the international Christian movement came when he went to Jerusalem in 1928 for the second of the great series of missionary conferences.

[2] F. A. Iremonger, *William Temple, Archbishop of Canterbury* (London: Oxford University Press, 1948), p. 378.

Many things had happened in the missionary world since 1910. During the first world war German missionaries had been interned or expelled from many territories. It was only by slow degrees that they were allowed to resume their work. Heroic efforts on the part of the newly formed International Missionary Council and its secretary, J. H. Oldham, were needed to prevent the sale of German missionary properties in West Africa to secular concerns. It was becoming clear, first to Dr. Oldham and gradually to many others, that Africa demanded far more thought and attention than had been paid to it by the Christian world. Men were becoming aware of a new enemy (secularism) that was undermining not only Christian faith but every kind of religious faith in the world. Eighteen years is a long interval; it seemed to many that the time had come for another great missionary assembly.

Jerusalem 1928 was a very different gathering from Edinburgh 1910. It was much smaller, though almost equally representative. And the same policy of gathering not only missionaries and mission board secretaries but also church leaders of eminence in various fields, and in particular a number of highly competent theologians, had been followed. It was in this last capacity that the services of William Temple had been specially sought.

As things turned out, this Conference gave him the opportunity to manifest, in notable measure, one of his special gifts. Here he was to display, for the first time, that special capacity, which called forth frequently the admiration, and sometimes the irritation, of his friends—the gift of finding the form of words in which two apparently irreconcilable points of view would find their reconciliation. Again and again during some heated discussion, the Archbishop would be seen to be quietly writing. At precisely the moment at which deadlock had been reached, he would rise and say, "I think that this is perhaps something approaching the kind of thing that we want to say." Again and again the heatedly disputing phalanxes would lay down their arms and find that the area of agreement between them was far greater than they had supposed. It has to be admitted that occasionally Temple's love of mental and verbal pyrotechnics carried him away, and that his agility produced a formula that was no more than a compromise between two really opposing views. But this was the rare exception. He had extraordinary gifts of penetration; while others were wrestling with surface questions, he could see through to the real issues the expression of which had eluded them. Above all God was the constant and unchanging background of his thinking. He was never interested in an immediate and pragmatic victory. On countless occasions those who sat with him felt that through his presence the subject of discussion had been lifted to an altogether higher level. The divine perspective had become apparent, and so Christians of really divergent outlook had been led to see the point at which their differing viewpoints could be brought together without dishonesty and without evasion.

Jerusalem 1928 gave ample scope for this irenic and diplomatic gift. This was the moment of the most acute tension between the more conservative and the more liberal wings of the missionary enterprise. The liberals had put forward certain ideas which, if accepted, would have meant a revolution in the whole conception of Christian missions. The task of the missionary would have been understood, not as trying to turn adherents of other faiths into Christians, but as co-operating with them in the discovery of the riches of their own faiths. On the other hand the new influences from the continent, associated with the name of Karl Barth, were already affecting some missionary circles. It seemed unlikely that the Conference would be able to issue any generally agreed statement on the central problems that lay before the missionary enterprise. To Temple was committed the task of preparing a draft of the message of the Conference.

In letters to his wife he has given some rather vivid pictures of how it was all done:

April 3, 1928. I was drafting all the morning, and seemed to be regarded as having done rather conspicuously my parlour trick of fitting everybody's pet point into a coherent document when they thought they were contradicting one another. . . . There is a draught in the hut this evening for some reason so my own candle is hopeless on the table. I have had to put it on the floor and write lying on the boards on my tummy.

April 4, 1928. . . . After tea I presented our report on the Message. . . . I seem to have written what opens the door for the progressives while perfectly satisfying the conservatives. As a matter of fact the *writing* was quite easy. We got the various sections so to state their own views that they were compatible with one another; and then it was only a matter of putting the bits together in the right order. . . . April 5. Our "Message" was unanimously accepted this morning by a standing vote, followed by silent prayer and thanksgiving. There is great jubilation, as it is thought to be good in itself, and there was apparently great anxiety that we should not be able to agree on anything substantial at all.[3]

As a matter of fact Temple has here rather underestimated the greatness of his own achievement. The disagreements were deep and serious; it was only his unshakable hold on essentials which made it possible to bring together the positive contributions of both wings.

To be appreciated, this classic message must be read in full. Here only a few brief extracts can be given as samples of its quality:

Our message is Jesus Christ. He is the revelation of what God is and of what man through Him may become. In Him we come face to face with the ultimate reality of the universe; He makes known to us God as our Father, perfect and infinite in love and in righteousness; for in Him we find God incarnate, the final yet ever unfolding revelation of the God in whom we live and move and have our being. . . . Our true and compelling motive lies in the very nature of the God to whom we have given our hearts. Since He is love, His very nature is to share. Christ is the expression in time of the eternal self-giving of the Father. Coming into fellowship with Christ we find in ourselves an over-mastering impulse to share Him with others. We are constrained by the love of Christ and by obedience to His last command. He Himself said, "I am come that they might have life, and that they might have it more abundantly," and our experience corroborates it. He has become life to us. We would share that life. . . .

[3] F. A. Iremonger, *op. cit.*, pp. 396-7.

We are persuaded that we and all Christian people must seek a more heroic practice of the Gospel. It cannot be that our present complacency and moderation are a faithful expression of the mind of Christ, and of the meaning of His Cross and Resurrection in the midst of the wrong and want and sin of our modern world.[4]

In the year before Jerusalem 1928 Temple had been present at the Lausanne Conference on Faith and Order. In the year after it, following upon the lamented death of Bishop Brent, he had been appointed chairman of the Continuation Committee of that movement. Few men more suitable for this office could have been found. Few leaders of that day were able to combine in the same degree as Temple the practical and the theoretical, an acute awareness of the actual situations of the church in the twentieth century with the constant reference of all things back to the basic principles of the life of the church in Jesus Christ.

Various committees of theologians had continued to work on the subjects left open or incompletely discussed at Lausanne 1927. Carefully planned volumes on the doctrine of grace (1932) and on the ministry of the church (1937) were published under the auspices of this committee. It had been taken as generally agreed that a second World Conference should be held at an interval of about ten years after the first. But these ten years revealed not so much a growing consensus as a deeper and more tragic sense of the reality of divisions. These is an almost plaintive note in Canon Leonard Hodgson's introduction to the volume on Edinburgh 1937. He recalled that in 1934

the provisional programme for 1937 . . . was severely criticised. It became clear that whereas in England and some other parts of the world, questions of the ministry and church order stood out as providing the most serious obstacles to unity, on the continent of Europe disagreements concerning the theological doctrines of Grace and the Word of God were felt to be of much more vital importance, while in America a most acute problem was presented by divisions based on psychological, social

[4] *Jerusalem Meeting Report* (London: International Missionary Council, 1928), I, 480, 485, 495.

and cultural factors and owing their origin to the course of historical development of the new world.[5]

These words were written in 1937; they might be taken as almost equally relevant to the state of the churches in 1960.

Once again Faith and Order met, this time in Edinburgh—more than four hundred delegates from 123 churches in almost every part of the world, and with rather better, though still wholly inadequate, representation from the younger churches.

By this time Temple had come to be so widely recognised as the towering ecumenical personality of the time that it was only natural that he should be chosen as chairman of the Conference and invited to preach the opening sermon. This sermon was most characteristic of Temple's thinking. While clear and open-eyed in its recognition of the reality and the sinfulness of division, its purpose throughout was to turn the eyes of men back to Christ, in whom alone is to be found healing for nations and churches:

The unity of the Church, on which our faith and hope is set, is grounded in the unity of God and the uniqueness of His redeeming act in Jesus Christ. . . . The unity of the Church of God is a perpetual fact; our task is not to create it, but to exhibit it. . . . The Church is not an association of men, each of whom has chosen Christ as Lord; it is a fellowship of men, each of whom Christ has united with Himself. The Christian faith and life are not a discovery or invention of men; they are not an emergent phase of the historical process; they are the gift of God. . . . It is not we who can heal the wounds in His body. We confer and deliberate, and that is right. But it is not by contrivance or adjustment that we can unite the Church of God. It is only by coming closer to Him that we can come nearer to one another. . . . We can help each other here, and learn from one another how to understand Him better. But it is towards Him that our eyes must be directed. Our discussion of our differences is a necessary preliminary; but it is preliminary and no more. Only when God has drawn us closer to Himself shall we

[5] *The Second World Conference on Faith and Order. Edinburgh 1937* (London: S. C. M. Press, 1938), p. 9.

be truly united together; and then our task will be, not to consummate our endeavour but to register His achievement.[6]

The Report of the Edinburgh Conference is a considerable document. It shows with what patience and diligence the delegates had searched out the issues of unity and difference. Perhaps at the end some of them may have felt that all their work had resulted only in bringing the differences more clearly and painfully to light, and the many footnotes and parentheses that various churches had felt it necessary to add show how easy it is for phrases to be used in varying senses by those of different traditions, and how difficult it is to arrive at an entirely satisfactory expression of Christian agreement. The report contained, however, one remarkable feature to which special reference must be made; this was an Affirmation of Union in allegiance to our Lord Jesus Christ, which was adopted by the Conference on August 18, 1937. This statement, covering only two pages in the report, sets out as clearly as any human words could do the deep longing of the churches for visible unity and their desire to go forward on the road to unity, whatever the difficulties in the way might be:

We are one in faith in our Lord Jesus Christ, the incarnate Word of God. We are one in allegiance to Him as Head of the Church, and as King of kings and Lord of lords. We are one in acknowledging that this allegiance takes precedence of any other allegiance that may make claims upon us.

This unity does not consist in the agreement of our minds or the consent of our wills. It is founded in Jesus Christ Himself, Who lived, died and rose again to bring us to the Father, and Who through the Holy Spirit dwells in His Church. We are one because we are all the objects of the love and grace of God, and called by Him to witness in all the world to His glorious Gospel. . . .

We pray that everywhere in a world divided and perplexed, men may turn to Jesus Christ our Lord, Who makes us one in spite of our divisions; that He may bind in one those who by many worldly claims are set at variance; and that the world

[6] *Op. cit.*, pp. 15, 17, 23.

may at last find peace and unity in Him; to Whom be glory for ever.[7]

The Conference had other things to do besides debating endlessly the problems of Christian union. It had before it a proposal for the formation of a World Council of Churches. For many years the movement for closer fellowship between the churches had been advancing along three separate and parallel lines—the International Missionary Council, Life and Work, and Faith and Order. There was considerable overlapping in personnel and an increasing feeling that this division of forces was both unnatural and harmful. We have already noted the strong missionary emphasis at Lausanne 1927. The movement called Life and Work had soon discovered the shallowness of the saying that doctrine divides while service unites. We cannot touch any question affecting Christian life, work, or witness without being driven back, in a very short time, on the fundamental problems of Christian theology. Life and Work itself had found it necessary to appoint a theological committee. The Faith and Order movement had found that "the search for unity is not made *in vacuo* but in relation to the Church's task in the world."[8] It was out of the gradually increasing sense of common concerns and the need of each movement for the others that the idea of a World Council of Churches was born.

It must not be supposed that the idea had an entirely easy passage at Edinburgh 1937 or anywhere else. Some felt that they were getting on very well as they were. Some were, even at that date, anxious lest a World Council of Churches might grow into a super-church and infringe the independence of the member-churches. Some in Faith and Order feared that the more liberal tendencies of certain churches which supported Life and Work might transform the Trinitarian basis of Faith and Order into a Unitarian form—an anxiety which we shall meet again later on. But in view of the steady support of Temple and other great leaders there could hardly be any doubt as to the way in which the vote would go. At a late hour on August

[7] *Op. cit.*, pp. 275-76.

[8] *The Ten Formative Years* (Geneva: World Council of Churches, 1948), p. 9.

11, 1937 the principle of a World Council was accepted by 112 votes to 19.

The details of the formation of the World Council will occupy us in another chapter. Here we are concerned only with one aspect of the development. The provisional committee of the World Council of Churches must have a chairman; there was no doubt in the minds of the leaders of the Christian world as to who that chairman should be. The result is stated laconically in one of the official publications of the Council: "The first meeting of this Provisional Committee was held at Utrecht on May 13, 1938. Archbishop William Temple was elected chairman." [9]

It was originally planned to hold the first Assembly of the World Council of Churches in 1941. Then came the cataclysm of the war. All thoughts of common Christian action had to be abandoned under the terrible and remorseless pressure of those years. Yet until 1942 Temple managed to retain a measure of contact with the secretariat in Geneva, and through it even with the churches in Germany. It was a great satisfaction to him to learn that his broadcast addresses and other statements had been welcomed by Christian leaders in neutral countries and in occupied lands, and that they had even been studied with appreciation and a great measure of agreement by leaders of the German churches. What man could do to keep alive the spirit of fellowship and oneness, Temple did.

And then tragedy fell upon the world. In 1942 Temple had become Archbishop of Canterbury. As days passed, he spoke with ever greater authority and a fuller ring of prophetic power in his voice. The Free Churches regarded him as "our Archbishop"; the man in the street knew that, if Lambeth spoke, he would hear something that would stir him with hope and courage for the future. And then quite unexpectedly, on October 26, 1944, William Temple died. Only once in our lifetime have the peoples of the British Commonwealth had to face an equal shock; that was on the morning in 1952 when they heard that King George VI had died peacefully during the night.

Although in this book I am writing so largely about my friends, I have kept the narrative strictly impersonal. On this

[9] *Ibid.* p. 11.

one page perhaps the personal note may intrude. Only a few days before Temple's death I had returned from India in ill-health. He had made an appointment for me to visit him and then had had to cancel it because of a particularly violent attack of gout. All that I could do was to go to Canterbury to represent the Church of India, Burma, and Ceylon at his funeral. The tide of victory was flowing, but the war was not yet over. Many of us had been separated from friends for long years, and the funeral seemed to take on almost the festive aspect of a gathering of old friends. We looked at one another a little askance, and then someone remarked, "The last thing that William would have wished would be that anyone should be gloomy at his funeral." It was perfectly true and fitting. Many years before he had himself written: "A funeral for me is not a parting, but merely the only way open to us of showing honour and love." It was appropriate that, gathered round his body, we sang the triumphant hymn, "The strife is o'er, the battle done, Alleluia."

When Temple died, he was mourned by literally millions of his fellow Christians. Thousands of people in all parts of the world felt that they had lost a personal friend. Those of us who were allowed to call him friend felt that we had been privileged to know the greatest Christian brought forth by the churches of Christ in our time and one of the greatest of all the Christian centuries.

VII. *Oxford* 1937

Let the Church Be the Church

INEVITABLY THIS BOOK HAS TO DEAL MOSTLY WITH THE SAYINGS and doings of Christians and churches, and perhaps a little too much with the activities of ecclesiastics. Yet it must never be forgotten that everything which happens in what we have now learned to call the ecumenical movement happens in relation to a changing world scene, of which the churches and their leaders are perhaps more conscious today than they have ever been before in the history of the church. We have seen how closely Stockholm 1925 was connected with the events and experiences of the First World War and how the bitter problem of "war-guilt" dogged the footsteps of the early ecumenical pioneers. As we follow the movement forward we are bound to find ourselves more and more involved in the great and often terrifying events that had been taking place far beyond the confines of the churches.

When the first Edinburgh Conference met in 1910, the churches were still in a mood of confidence and hope. A tremendous epoch of progress and expansion lay behind them, and there seemed no particular reason to think that a similar epoch would not lie ahead. It was true that the defeat of Russia by Japan in 1905 had indicated to those with eyes to see that a startling displacement of power was taking place and that the unchallenged supremacy of the West had now been sharply challenged, but few had any premonition of all that was to follow and of the series of disasters in which all the familiar outlines of the political and the ecclesiastical scene were to disappear.

The first war had revealed the thinness of the Christian veneer in all the so-called Christian countries and had permanently shaken the authority and prestige of "the Christian West" in all the non-Christian parts of the world. The Russian revolution had, for the time being, torn away from the Christian world a great and ancient group of churches and had let loose on the world an incalculable force that seemed bent on destroying forever every kind of religious faith. And then after years of restlessness in Germany Adolf Hitler came to power in 1933.

It is fashionable today to see nothing but evil in the Nazi regime from the start. It requires an effort of imagination to recall what that regime looked like to those who lived under it in the early days. Hitler cleaned up a great deal of evil and corruption. Witness the Swedes, who suffered as the purveyors of pornographic literature in Germany escaped over the frontier and set up their nefarious trade in Sweden. At a time when unemployment was soaring, Hitler gave the Germans work and food, and men will put up with a great deal from a government that gives them these two things. More than anything else he gave back to that great and proud people a sense of personal and national dignity—Germany was no longer to be the pawn of competing victors; it would again count for something in the councils of the nations. Even wise and good Christians did not immediately realise the vastness of the problem by which they had been confronted.

For, in fact, Hitler had raised what is always the question of life or death for the church. Are state, community, and nation the supreme authorities? Or is there a point at which even the patriotic Christian has to be prepared to say "No" to the rulers of his country, on behalf of a greater and more lasting good? A Roman Catholic writer has summed it up as the problem of the survival of the church in a community which recognizes no formal limits, but which spreads its authority over the whole of life and claims to be the source and goal of every human activity.

These large-scale political events represented visible dangers to the church. There were working at the same time other and less obvious forces, which perhaps in the end would have even more serious consequences in undermining the life of the churches and weakening their hold on the minds and wills of men.

First, there was secularism. From the beginning there has been a certain conflict, or at least incompatibility, between man's sense of loyalty to God and his absorption in the daily concerns of work and home and society. When did that higher loyalty begin to disappear, as man's confidence in himself grew, and the concerns of that which can be seen and felt and touched began to seem all-important as contrasted with those things which may be eternal but are not seen? It is hard to fix on any one particular date. Already in the Middle Ages we can see something of the tension. But there can be little doubt that the process was greatly helped forward by the movement of the eighteenth century known in Germany as the *Aufklaerung* and in England as the Enlightenment. This was the age of Reason. Man in the days of his infancy had needed revelation to help him forward in this difficult world. But now that he is grown up, he will find his own way, will master himself and his surroundings, and will be the creator of his own new world. Such ways of thinking were helped forward by the industrial revolution, by the wonderful discoveries of physical science, and by the harnessing of these discoveries to human welfare in countless ways. We of the middle of the twentieth century are secularized, perhaps far more than we ourselves know, in all our ways of thinking and feeling.

The nature of this process and its end were acutely summed up in a book which appeared just at the time of which we are now writing:

> Men have preferred the material to the spiritual. They have sought the heaven upon earth, which they believed that their own efforts could enable them to create. They are captivated by utopias which hold out the promise of comfort and prosperity. They live by theories which blind them to the realities of human existence. They are no longer able to see the ultimate facts which encompass man's life—the realities of death, sin, judgment and God.[1]

If men have come to think and live in this way, they are not likely to be much interested in the church. It is not that they hate the church or wish to attack it; it is all right for those who

[1] J. H. Oldham and W. A. Visser 't Hooft, *The Church and its Function in Society* (Geneva: The World Council of Churches, 1937), p. 111.

like that kind of thing, a spare-time activity for those who have time to spare. The problem is that the church and all it stands for, the whole spiritual dimension, has come to seem supremely irrelevant. There was a time when men believed passionately in these things and were prepared to burn one another alive for not believing exactly in the right way. Now we do not do such things. It might be better if we did, and as we shall see later, the renewal of the church in Germany came precisely when the opposing powers had to take the church seriously, and when men were prepared both to kill and to die because questions of faith had once again come to seem supremely important.

What were Christians to do in such a time as this? We shall find two words that recur almost monotonously in the literature of the time. The first is "reaffirmation." The second is "the church."

But what was to be reaffirmed? Merely to say over again all the things that the church had been saying for so long would cut no ice. Good ideas are always true, whoever may happen to announce them. And good advice is not very welcome to those who think they know better anyhow. But in the years after the first war it came to seem to many in the church that they had something new to say, something really very old but so long forgotten that it came with the accents of new truth. What matters is not what men think, but what has happened. In Jesus Christ certain things *happened.* As a result of the things that happened, or to put it more theologically, of the things that God did in the death and resurrection of Jesus Christ, the whole being of the universe, the relation of men to themselves and to one another and to the God who made them, has been changed. We live literally in new heavens and a new earth.

During the war years, a young Swiss pastor of liberal outlook had found that his message had nothing to say to men and women in a time of desperate crisis. As he pondered the world situation and the Bible, his outlook was changed. In 1918 there came from the press Karl Barth's *Commentary on the Epistle to the Romans,* a strange shapeless work in which, for all its chaotic form, countless men and women found the authentic accent of the voice of God speaking in modern terms. After reading this book, a German pastor summed up the experience of countless others: "Now I can preach." For forty years Barth has been one of the great teachers and prophets of the Christian world, and even those who least agree with him have had to take him most seriously. His message crossed the Atlantic; in different and characteristic form Reinhold Niebuhr and his followers, in what has come to be known as Neo-Orthodoxy, began to set forth the same doctrine of challenge, renewal, and reaffirmation.

The nineteenth century had been the great age of individualism —a man's business is to make the best of himself and to get as near the top of the tree as he can by his own unaided efforts. This was the gospel of American greatness, and "From Log-cabin to White House" was the theme of some written and a great many unwritten biographies. But as early as the end of the nineteenth century even in America people were beginning to wonder whether this was the whole of the gospel for mankind. With the industrial revolution and mass society new and more formidable pressures have been brought to bear on man. Immense powers are at work in the world, which the ordinary man can hardly understand, which he cannot influence, and yet which determine the shape and pattern of his life. A slight change in the markets in London and Chicago, and thousands of workers may be thrown out of work in Tokyo. What then of individual rights and freedom? These are great realities, but can they be more than pleasant words in a world in which man seems to be the plaything of circumstances far beyond his own control? In such a world man cannot stand alone; what he needs above all else is community.

In the days of individualism Christians had been almost as individualistic as anyone else; the faith seemed to be concerned with individual salvation or with the reinforcement of the efforts of the individual to make himself. The church appeared as little more than a convenience, in which the individual might or might not find the spiritual or ethical help of which he stood in need. But now, as the church like the individual was threatened by these dark and hardly distinguishable forces, by the dimension of the "daemonic," the idea of community began to re-emerge from the shadows; not now one of the many communities that men can and do rightly make for themselves, but a divine community founded by God himself in Christ, a community which has always been there though often forgotten, a reality which ought to be able to speak to man's condition in dark days, and in which man, all men of whatever degree, ought to be able to find a home.

There is no rule as to the holding of ecumenical conferences; empirically, it has been found that ten years is as good an interval as any other. It was clear that Stockholm 1925 had to be followed up. By 1934 it had been decided that another conference, dealing with much the same themes but relating them to the changed situation, should be held. Those who reached this conclusion were extraordinarily fortunate in their choice of the man who was to be chief planner of the next great conference on Life and Work.

Joseph Houldsworth Oldham was born of a Scottish family in 1874 but has spent most of his life in England and has become an Anglican. After a short period of service with the Y.M.C.A. in India Oldham returned to Britain to study theology. Part of his studies were carried out in Germany, and a thorough knowledge of German and an unusual alertness to the movements of thought on the continent have remained with him ever since. His mind is always moving on the frontiers of thought, trying to ascertain where the next great problems will confront mankind and getting there long before the ordinary man has even become aware that a problem exists.

Real Life Is Meeting is the title of one of Oldham's books. A better summary of the man could hardly be wished for. He has never wished to appear on public platforms and has acquired no reputation as an orator. For this reason Joe and the extraordinary part he has played in ecumenical development remain almost unknown to those who depend for their knowledge on the public press and the reports of great ecumenical utterances. Oldham's strength is in personal relationships. Hampered from early years by deafness, which any other man would have allowed to cut him off from the fellowship of his kind, he has managed for more than fifty years to gather round him one generation after another of younger men and women, whom he has stimulated to think, to reach out to the new ideas, to be aware of the future just as he has been himself. "Joe thinks that all the really important ecumenical decisions are made over a table in the corner of the dining-room at the Athenaeum'' (the club in London to which a great many bishops belong), was the kindly and not altogether inaccurate remark of one who knows him well.

But there is another side of Oldham that must not be forgotten. He has written a number of books and one best seller; the best seller is called *A Devotional Diary.* This little book has gone through edition after edition. It is a searching challenge to the reader to be honest with himself as to what he really does about the life of prayer, as distinct from talking about it, and offers him intelligent help in the way of doing better. Such a book could have grown out of nothing but long years of effort and experiment on the part of the writer. Ecumenical affairs are largely concerned with speeches, committees, and arguments. So much time is taken up by these unavoidable things that it is easy for the participants to forget that it really does matter whether men and women pray or not. It has been of incalculable value to the whole movement to have at its heart one man who never for a moment has forgotten this foundation truth.

But we have not yet come to that particular gift which has made Oldham so creative in ecumenical affairs. He has shown himself the greatest organizer of international conferences who has ever lived. This gift was first shown in connection with Edinburgh 1910, when Oldham, then only thirty-five years old, was in charge of all that immense process of preliminary study which made Edinburgh the best prepared of all the great conferences up to that date. Now in preparation for Oxford 1937 his gifts were displayed to even greater advantage.

Experts in all directions, including many laymen of distinction who had never heard the word ''ecumenical,'' were pressed into the service. Papers were written and circulated. Comments from other experts came in, sometimes only a few lines, sometimes lengthy and careful documents that themselves deserved to rank as ''papers.'' In all more than three hundred collaborators took part in the work, rather too many perhaps from the English-speaking world, but for this the political situation of that time gives a ready explanation. A climate of thinking was being created; men and women were getting to know one another and gradually to make clear to themselves and others the kind of problems that were pressing on the church from every side. Oldham knew well that no ecumenical conference can be prepared in less than three years; by 1937 he was ready. The results of this long period of gestation were to be published in six volumes.

It is unfortunate that during the Second World War almost the whole stock of these volumes was destroyed in the bombing of London; they have become in consequence something of an ecumenical rarity, and are far less widely known than they deserve. But even to read through the names of the contributors is an exciting ecumenical education. A volume which contains essays by H. H. Farmer, now of Cambridge, Reinhold Niebuhr of New York, and the Archbishop of York (Temple) is likely to provide stimulating reading. In 1937 not so many people knew who Paul A. Tillich was, but Oldham had found him out. Dr. H. Lilje was not then the famous Bishop of Hanover. And it comes as almost a shock to read among the names that of John Foster Dulles. More than half of those who contributed are still living; they would probably all agree that a quiet and firm ecumenical education under the hand of Joe Oldham was one of the most stimulating, though occasionally infuriating, experiences that they had ever passed through.

And so at last, after this long period of preparation, they met in Oxford in July 1937, about 435 representatives from many races and churches. Nothing could be more boring than an account of conference after conference, each in its main outlines very much like all the rest. Yet each has its own special features, and the record is not complete unless some attempt is made to detach these from the general jungle of ecumenical history.

The first thing that is likely to strike the reader of the Oxford records is the stress laid on worship. The times of prayer and worship in St. Mary's Church seem to have left a deeper impression on those present than almost anything else. That this was so was due in the main to one man and one only—Canon Cockin, the rector of St. Mary's. Dr. Cockin, commonly known as George because his names are Frederick Arthur, had, like Oldham, served for a short period in India, and then for a considerably longer period with the Student Christian Movement of Britain.

In 1946, very unwillingly, he accepted promotion to the bishopric of Bristol. Unlike many others who have made similar resolutions, he has adhered sternly to the decision never to speak without careful preparation. Over the years, without any special gifts of eloquence, he has exercised the quiet influence of a humble and faithful man—his entry in *Who's Who* carries modesty and taciturnity almost to excess—and of a wise counsellor to many friends. Perhaps he has never had greater moments than those in which he directed the worship of the Oxford Conference.

Ecumenical worship presents a whole range of insoluble problems. There is no common language. Those present range from the Friends who have no liturgical tradition at all and are accustomed to worship in silence, to the Orthodox who are used to the splendor and pageantry of ancient liturgies, and have never even considered the horrible possibility that a woman might be called to lead in public worship. It is no easy thing to create a unity in worship and adoration in an ecumenical setting. Cockin worked tirelessly with the various leaders, helping them to see what could be done with so motley a throng assembled to worship in the unfamiliar setting of an English Gothic church. The success of his efforts comes out more than once in the reports:

> In the periods of silence there was often an overpowering sense that things were happening in the spiritual world, and that in the coming years one might expect to see in the breaking out of life in countless directions in answer to the prayers that were being offered together to God.[2]

The German Evangelical churches were not represented at the Conference. Leaders in those churches had taken an active part in the preparations, but at the last moment the government of Hitler made impossible the attendance of any member of the official delegation. There were present three members of the small Free Churches which had managed to make a deal with Hitler; their presence only emphasised the absence of the others. If Hitler had deliberately intended to draw the attention of

[2] *The Churches Survey their Task,* pp. 10-11.

the world to the nature of the German church struggle, still very imperfectly understood outside Germany, he could not have done better. The Conference marked its sense of the solemnity of the occasion by sending a message of brotherly sympathy to the churches in Germany.

If one predominant note is to be chosen out from the many pages of the report, it should probably be that of the dignity of man as man. It was this that the delegates felt to be threatened by so many things in modern life—by the squalid conditions of overcrowding in the cities, by inequality of economic and educational opportunity, above all by the totalitarian state with its unmitigated demands for a total surrender of the human will to supposedly higher powers. On all these things the Conference tried to lay down the measured judgment of the Christian churches.

It is curious that the phrase, "Let the Church be the Church," which has always been specially associated with Oxford 1937, does not occur in its official reports. It seems to be due to the mind and invention of John A. Mackay, at one time a missionary in Latin America, later president of Princeton Seminary and chairman of the International Missionary Council, and one of the outstanding orators of the ecumenical cause. The phrase occurs in the original draft of the report on "The Universal Church and the World of Nations," of which Mackay was chairman; there is every reason to suppose that the words actually came from his mind and his pen.

What do they mean? How can the church be anything but the church? The events of the day had lent a tragic significance to precisely this question. Man lives in many worlds—the church, the family, his place of employment, the state, the wider world of nations. What is the relationship of these to one another and of the church to them all? Many different answers have been given. In the Middle Ages church and state were practically identical, and the church claimed the right to lay down man's duties and responsibilities in all the worlds in which he might be called to live. In 1937 it seemed to the delegates to the Conference that the churches in Russia had arrived at a manner of living which depended on a total separation of two worlds. The church may exist if it confines its activities wholly to the concerns of the other world (which from the communist point of view is a wholly nonexistent world) provided that it leaves to the government all the concerns of this world (which from the communist point of view is the only real world). The Nazi government of Hitler proclaimed the full satisfaction of all man's needs and destinies in the service of the state. America proclaimed the legal separation of church and state, yet recognised the constant overlapping of the concerns of the churches and those of the state.

What Oxford 1937 was concerned about was the recovery of the prophetic function of the church—that faculty of discernment and of pungent utterance in relation to current concerns which we find in the great prophets of the Old Testament. But how is this function to be exercised in the modern world?

William Temple once remarked that when people say that the church ought to do something, they usually mean that the bishops ought to say something. One of those deeply concerned in the preparations for the Conference wrote that the genuine utterances of the mind of the church must not be confused with statements which merely expressed the wishful thinking of a minority of the members of the churches—a warning which has not always been taken as seriously as it might have been. Yet the dilemma is real and intense. If in times of crisis the churches say nothing, they may seem to be indifferent to the needs and concerns of those who suffer and of the great majority of the human race. If they keep themselves to broad generalisations, they may produce nothing but a string of platitudes, such as any fairly intelligent minister of the church could produce in his study on a Saturday afternoon. If they descend into the details of immediate situations, they are likely to be rebuked by the experts for laying down the law on matters which they know nothing about—sometimes with good reason, for the churches as such have no expert knowledge of intricate questions of economic principle.

Yet even when all this has been recognized, the churches are not necessarily condemned to silence. It is not always possible to say what is right; quite often it is possible to say what is wrong. After all the law under the Old Covenant was expressed in terms of "Thou shalt not. . . ." The church itself is under grace, but it may have words to say to those who are still under the law. The great utterances of the prophets had to do largely with those things that ought not to have happened and ought not to be allowed, amid a people that called itself the people of God. If the churches courageously fulfill their function of saying what ought not to be, this is by no means a negligible contribution to the well-being of the world.

Sometimes the individual lay Christian sees things more clearly than wise conferences of Christian leaders. At the high table of a Cambridge college, conversation had turned on the new Germany, and a young German guest was trying to defend Hitler's third Reich and all its doings. An eminent historian, usually of quiet demeanor and measured speech, suddenly broke in—"Not many years will have passed before your Hitler will have gone to the place where he belongs, and that is hell." Oxford 1937 did not speak quite so abruptly as this; yet it showed itself well aware of the many evils that frustrate and thwart and distort the life of men.

But this was a Christian Conference. Beyond the nay lies the yea, and this too found expression:

> There is no legal, political, or economic system so bad or so good as to absolve individuals from the responsibility to transcend its requirements by acts of Christian charity. Institutional requirements necessarily prescribe only the minimum. Even in the best possible social system they can only achieve general standards in which the selfishness of the human heart is taken for granted and presupposed. But the man who is in Christ knows a higher obligation, which transcends the requirements of justice—the obligation of a love which is the fulfilling of the law.[3]

Twenty years later we are still trying to spell out the full meaning of these wise and Christian words.

[3] *Ibid.*, p. 94.

VIII

Paton and Kraemer the Younger Churches Arrive

ONCE A GREAT INTERNATIONAL CHRISTIAN ASSEMBLY HAS MET, recorded its views, and dispersed, there may seem to be no particular reason why it should ever meet again. Yet, as we have seen, all the main Christian movements of recent years have shown a tendency to call great assemblies about once in ten years. Edinburgh 1910 was a splendid demonstration of the strength of the Christian cause in the world. Jerusalem 1928 had been a much smaller meeting, perhaps harder working just because it was smaller. But there was no general agreement in the missionary world as to whether anything would be gained by the calling of another such general meeting. Had anything really new emerged in the Christian situation, and could not the routine work be carried out efficiently and far more cheaply by the regular committees of the International Missionary Council?

But unobserved by many, something new had emerged.

"The great new fact of our time." So spoke Archbishop William Temple on the occasion of his enthronement in Canterbury Cathedral. Few slogans of modern times have been so extensively misunderstood and misapplied as this. It has been supposed by many that the Archbishop was referring to what we now commonly call the ecumenical movement, or even to the formation of the World Council of Churches, of the Provisional Committee of which he was himself at that time chairman. This is not in the least what he was talking about; he was referring to the growth over two centuries of a genuinely world-wide Christian community, as the result of the success of the missionary work carried on by all the Christian churches in all parts of the world. It is literally true that, in the twentieth century, for the first time Christianity has become a universal religion. Scholars tell us that, alone among the great religions of the world, the Christian faith has had built into its texture from the beginning the claim to universality. Alone among the great religions it has found means to make itself a universal faith.

Of course, the limits within which this is true must be kept carefully in mind. It is very far from being the case that everyone in the world has become Christian or has even heard the name of Jesus Christ. That is not the sense in which the word universality is used. It is, however, the fact that the gospel has been preached in almost every part of the world and has won converts from the members of almost every race. Until recently the kingdom of Nepal, on the troubled frontier between India and China, was a closed country where no Christian work was permitted; now it is open, and a variety of Christian agencies have found their way there. Only Tibet and Afghanistan still keep their doors firmly closed, and even in Afghanistan there are at least the worshiping companies of resident Europeans and Americans, though no direct preaching to the people of the country is allowed. Most of the Eskimo in Canada are now Christians of one church or another. Pygmies in the eternal rain forest of Africa have heard and accepted the Word. At the same time every other known form of religious faith has yielded some converts to Christianity—few from the higher faiths such as Islam and Zoroastrianism, very many from among animists and adherents of other simpler faiths.

This is the new fact. Supporters of the missionary enterprise were aware of these things and in their enthusiasm sometimes exaggerated the results that had actually been achieved. But even they were slow to grasp the significance of what was happening. What was the status of these new groups of Christians that were coming into existence in so many countries of the world? How were they to make their voice heard in the general Christian chorus? What influence could they be expected to exert on the development of the Christian cause in the world?

Before 1910 these questions had hardly been asked. The new Christians were "converts" of the missionary societies. They had been introduced to various forms of Western Christianity, which they had faithfully accepted exactly as taught to them, and without any clear discrimination between what was inherent in the gospel and what was simply part of the national tradition of the particular set of missionaries who had come to them. In many cases the church to which they belonged was simply a part of the church in the homeland, with no status or independence of its own. Thus, for example, the Anglican Church in India was until 1930 legally "the Church of England in India." It had to use exactly the English Prayer Book without deviation. Bishop Cotton's beautiful prayer for India had been sanctioned for use in church services, but so strictly were the rules kept that it was not printed in the Prayer Book. It was printed separately and pasted on to the inner cover of the Prayer Books sent out in the languages of India. Many similar examples could be given of the limitations imposed on the growth and freedom of the younger churches by such archaic and unnecessary rules.

Two disastrous effects followed. The first was that on the whole the Christians of these newer churches lived in a state of contented dependence on the missionaries, who had done everything for them, decided everything for them, and in a number of cases paid everything for them. The second was that inevitably and almost everywhere in Asia and Africa the church had a foreign look. Little Indian choirboys, in not always very clean surplices, sang the Psalms to Anglican chants in languages whose rhythm suffers excruciatingly under such treatment. Church buildings, church services, ways of living were all related to a civilization six thousand miles away and not to the daily life of the people and to their responsibility for the non-Christians who lived round about them.

It was clear to the keenest and most thoughtful minds that this state of things could not go on very much longer.

In the first place there was nationalism. In 1921 M. K. Gandhi, "Mahatmaji" to millions of his fellow countrymen, came back from South Africa to put himself at the head of the Indian national movement. China was passing through a period of violent anti-foreign feeling. Japan was highly conscious of its status as a great world power which had rendered conspicuous service to the Allied cause in the First World War. In the earlier years of these movements Christians had, on the whole, kept their distance from them. They were not much interested in politics, and they could not approve of some of the methods that were being followed by the more passionate supporters of nationalism. But it was already becoming clear that this stream was growing into a torrent that would carry all before it, that the younger churches could not continue to exist as frail colonies of the West, and that they must find roots in their own countries, in relation to the new sense of national pride, if they were to continue to have any existence at all in the new epoch of national freedom and independence.

But all this was not the chief concern of the best thinkers in the missionary world. We have already had occasion to note the rise of a new consciousness of the significance of the church and a new interest in the theology of it. Here was the heart of the problem. What is a church? Can a group of Indian or Chinese Christians living in dependence on a missionary society, which itself may have no very clearly defined relationship to the church, be called or regarded as a church? Is not some fundamental rethinking needed? Must not these younger churches have in their sphere the same sort of freedom as the politicians are demanding on the national front? Must they not have liberty to express the Christian faith in their own way, and if necessary fall into some heresies in the process of doing so? Must they not be free to consider what parts of their own national heritage in music, literature, and the arts can be Christianized and brought into the life of the church? Can we expect ever to have leaders in these churches, unless we give full freedom to the best men and women in them to take responsibility, to make their own decsions, to make their own mistakes?

Fifty years ago many of these questions had hardly been asked, and even today there are parts of the world in which, though correct answers may have been given in theory, practice is not yet determined by the new insights that are the fruit of these years. That this is so is evident from a brief consideration of the representation of the younger churches at the great international gatherings that have come before us in our survey. At Edinburgh 1910 only eighteen Asians and Africans were present, and not one of these had come as the representative of a church; all were there either by appointment from a missionary society or by special nomination of the Conference committee. At

Jerusalem 1928 things were better, though the membership of the Conference was overwhelmingly Western. It is significant that it was in this period that the term "younger churches," now so familiar to us all, first began to be regularly heard. But it was clear that things must move much faster and that to some extent the lead must be given from the top.

One of those who had thought most deeply about the younger church problem was John R. Mott. It seemed to him that the time had come for another general assembly of the missionary forces, and that this time it must be quite clearly the great council of the younger churches. Under his guidance the International Missionary Council accepted the principle that, at its next great meeting, half of the delegates must be nationals of the countries which they came to represent, and that half of them must be under the age of thirty-five. This was not to be a gathering of reverend seniors, distilling wisdom from the many years in which their beards had grown. It was to be in large part a collection of young men and women from East and West, some perhaps angry, all eager, and in general more ready for adventure than the majority of those who come to the great synods of the church.

Shortly before the Jerusalem Conference John R. Mott had found an ideal lieutenant—William Paton. "A bulldog." That, I think, is the phrase that is likely to come to the mind of anyone seeing, for the first time, his picture, as it hangs in the entrance hall of the World Council of Churches or reproduced as the frontispiece to his life by Margaret Sinclair. A square, determined face, speaking perhaps of Scottish ancestry and Presbyterian resolution, of a man not given to any display of easy emotion, accustomed to reflect long and deeply, and then to carry out quietly and efficiently what he had resolved to do. It is, in brief, the face of one of the wise men of the earth. His biographer, comparing him with his great leader Mott, notes a similarity of outlook in the two men:

> the openness of mind to the Will of God, the approach to a difficulty not as an obstacle looming darkly ahead, but as something to be examined for the clue, obscured and embedded

though it might be, to a next move in a particular plan of advance.[1]

Many things had combined to fit Paton for his special service in the International Missionary Council. He had come up through the British Student Movement and had served it in various capacities. But at a time when others were finding their way with difficulty through a period of liberal confusion in which many of the great landmarks of the Christian faith seemed to be disappearing, his mind settled gradually and patiently into a firm and unshakable faith in the reality of the incarnation, of the fact that God Almighty had actually lived and worked on earth as a man. In these years Paton became one of the speakers to whom students listened with the greatest pleasure. If he was on the program, you knew that you would have to listen to something fairly exacting, to a speaker who never tried to emphasize his point by any tricks of oratory, but who always had a good and solid point, backed up by wide reading and exact thought.

Then came a call to serve with the Y.M.C.A. in India, a country which Paton had come to know and love during the First World War. This was almost immediately changed into something larger and more exciting. John R. Mott's travels after Edinburgh 1910 had resulted in the formation of a number of national missionary councils, one of the best of which was the council that served the churches in India. In 1922 the decision was reached to transform this into the National Christian Council of India, Burma and Ceylon, with a permanent and full-time staff. What's in a name? Nothing, perhaps, but perhaps very much. Here the change of name and structure meant a revolution in thought and practice. It had been decided that half the membership of the new council must be Indian. One who served both before and after the change remarked that, if you compared the two man by man, unquestionably the earlier council was the abler, but that equally unquestionably the later was the better council. It was more Indian, and therefore, better

[1] Margaret Sinclair, *William Paton* (London: S. C. M. Press, 1949), p. 17. When Dr. Garbett, Archbishop of York, heard of Paton's death in 1943, he recorded in his diary the comment: "If he had been an Anglican, he would have been one of the Archbishops." Charles Smyth, *Cyril Foster Garbett* (London: Hodder and Stoughton, 1959), p. 460.

able both to discern the signs of the times and to help the churches to measure up to their responsibilities and opportunities in the New India.

Paton was just the man to make such a council work. He loved India and Indians. He was deeply sympathetic with national aspirations and with the perplexities of the young, who often found it difficult to reconcile their Christian loyalties with their new vision of greatness for their people. He was everywhere, knew everyone from the Viceroy down to the simple village catechist. And everywhere he bred the spirit of understanding, sympathy, and good will.

It was India's loss and the world's gain, when he was called back from India to the London office of the I.M.C. Years passed and wisdom grew. This was the man who was chosen to organise the third great missionary assembly of the churches.

The difficulty in finding a place for the meeting reflects the unsettlement of the times. First it was to be at Kowloon—to the indignation of the Chinese, since Kowloon, though it is on the mainland of China, is in British hands as part of the colony of Hong Kong. Chinese insistence got this changed to Hangchow, "Heaven Below," a city the beauty of which Chinese and foreigners vie with one another in extolling. But this was not to be. Japanese aggression had disrupted the normal life of China, and it was felt that prudence indicated yet another change. Finally, the choice fell on the Christian College at Tambaram near Madras—to the bitter disappointment of one delegate from India, who had to wait ten more years for his first visit to China.

This great college had existed for the best part of a century in the city of Madras and had only just moved to the extensive new site eighteen miles from the city. It is a lovely place, well planted with trees so arranged by the devotion and genius of a member of the staff that something is always in flower. It has educated many of the greatest leaders of the Indian Church and influenced many of the most notable among Indians who have not become Christians. It has been served by many great men. Conspicuous among those of recent years is Alec Boyd, who retired from the principalship shortly before this book was written, after thirty-five years of service in India, during which he acquired the reputation of being one of the best loved missionaries of any country or of any time.

So here we all arrived in the early days of December, 1938. And what a collection it was! Here were many of our old friends. Inevitably the chairman was John R. Mott, now seventy-three years old, but full of fire—"I have never heard the old man to better advantage," remarked one delegate after Mott's closing speech. One of the speakers was Bishop Azariah. But there were many new faces as well. England had sent Dr. Garbett, then Bishop of Winchester and later Archbishop of York. Those who knew him well believed that the great release of new life which made Garbett, in his closing years, the chief spokesman of the Church of England dated from the shock of his encounter with the younger churches at Tambaram. Theologians of eminence came from many countries, among them Professor Farmer, now of Cambridge, and Dr. H. P. Van Dusen, now President of Union Theological Seminary, New York. Paton had worked hard to secure the best possible representation and had not always worked on conventional lines. Two of the chairmen of sections were almost unknown young men, both then under the age of forty, one of them now well known as Count S. C. van Randwijck, General Secretary of the Board of Missions of the Netherlands Reformed Church.

But, of course, the great thrill was the arrival of the delegates of the younger churches. "This *is* the Holy Catholic Church," one delegate was moved to say to himself, as he saw them all assembled in the first plenary session. And among them all pride of place went to the Chinese. Their situation was delicate in the extreme. Japan and China were not openly at war, but China was already suffering all the agonies of invasion—and the Japanese were also at Tambaram. By the dignity of their bearing, their calm refusal to allow themselves to be embittered, their individual distinction as thinkers, speakers, and simply as Christians, the Chinese won for themselves the affectionate admiration of the whole assembly. Never again would it be necessary for younger church leaders to claim equality with their brethren from the West; it had been already granted by acclamation. For a long time it had been doubtful whether any delegates from Germany would reach the Conference. But this time the disaster of Oxford 1937 was not repeated, and one British delegate recalls with pleasure that during the first four days of the Conference he sat between Prelate Karl Hartenstein of the Church of Wurttemberg and Gerhard Brennecke, now General Secretary of the Berlin Missionary Society.

The Conference had met. What was it going to do? First, it had to face a theological problem of no mean magnitude: What is to be the attitude of the Christian to the other religions of the world? How far can he accept them as being in some measure a manifestation of the truth of God?

At Jerusalem 1928 the liberal influence had been very strong. A plea had been made that all religions should recognise that their real enemy is secularism, and that they should all unite to defend the spiritual interpretation of the world. This was carried even further by a famous book, *Re-thinking Missions,* published in 1932 as the outcome of the survey of missions made by a group of American laymen. Here it was plainly stated that the business of the missionary was not to supplant the ancient religions, but to co-operate with the best elements in them. What was Tambaram 1938 to say? Shortly before the Conference met, a rock of the largest size had been cast into the already not very calm waters of the missionary world.

And so we meet one of the most remarkable of all those who had gathered to spend Christmas together in South India—Hendrik Kraemer. Everything in the career of this outstanding man is paradoxical. He has never been a missionary; he went to Indonesia as an expert in languages and Bible translation on behalf of the Bible Society of the Netherlands. Yet no living man has exercised a deeper influence on missionary thinking. He is a layman. But no minister has had more to do with shaping the new pattern for the life of the Dutch Reformed Church. He is not a theologian. Yet he has read more theology than many of those who make it their profession, and by his writings and his work as Director of the Ecumenical Institute near Geneva he has influenced the theological thinking of many of the leaders in the younger generation.

As preparation for the Conference, delegates had been asked to read, not as for Oxford 1937 a sheaf of papers, but one single large volume, Kraemer's *The Christian Message in a non-Chris-*

tian World. This is by far the greatest of Kraemer's writings. It is a magisterial survey of the whole situation of the Christian world face to face with the non-Christian peoples and religions. Nothing comparable to it has appeared so far in this century; it is perhaps unlikely that anything equal to it will appear in the next fifty years. In his book Kraemer said a decisive and emphatic *no* to all the affirmations of the liberals. We may rightly say that God has somehow and somewhere spoken in the non-Christian religions, though it is difficult to be precise and to say when and where. But in Jesus Christ God has acted, has spoken his final and decisive word. Nothing in any other religion is the least like this. From the non-Christian faiths to biblical realism there is no direct way. Given the choice between continuity and discontinuity, we must opt every time in favor of the idea of discontinuity. Passage from a non-Christian religion to faith in Christ must always be of the nature of death and rebirth and can be nothing else. Such a bare summary cannot do justice to the riches and force of the original; it can only indicate the lines of the controversy.

And fierce and full the controversy raged! Naturally there were at Tambaram representatives of the older liberalism, to whom Kraemer's doctrine was anathema. And even many of those who were prepared to go a long way with him could not accept all his more violent statements in their entirety. The controversy is still with us, and we cannot follow its details here. Suffice it to say that, in a measure, though not entirely, the movement of Christian thought over twenty years has been in the direction of Kraemer rather than away from him, and many of the things which shocked opinion at Tambaram would seem a good deal less startling if said today.

In addition, however, to its main topic Tambaram 1938 in its sixteen sections made a wide and efficient survey of all the problems of the younger churches in their approach to full manhood within the fellowship of Christ. In two directions it struck the prophetic note, though it is to be regretted that not all its prophecies have yet come to fulfilment.

If the younger churches are ever to stand on their own feet, it is essential that they should have ordained ministers as well trained as the representatives of the older churches who come to work among them, though the training given in these younger churches need not necessarily follow exactly the lines that have become traditional in the West. The Conference affirmed that "the present condition of theological education is one of the greatest weaknesses in the whole Christian enterprise" and sounded a clarion call for improvement. But in view of the recent development of interest in lay ministries in the church, it is noteworthy that this section at Tambaram opened its report on the ordained ministry with a classic statement on the priestly character of the church as a whole:

The Church is the body of Christ. In all its work of ministering, whether priestly, pastoral or prophetic, it is animated by the life of the risen and ascended Christ, who is at once the great High Priest, the Chief Shepherd of souls, and the eternal Word of God. This ministry is committed to us as a function of the whole body of Christ and cannot therefore be claimed exclusively by individuals or by one order within the church. Nevertheless from the time of the Apostles there have been special orders and ministries in the Church, given by God, for the perfecting of the saints unto the work of ministering, unto the building up of the body of Christ.[2]

Far less has been done than should have been done to follow up the recommendations of this section. Yet some things have been done. The progress of work for the improvement of theological training in the younger churches can be to some extent followed in two notable books, *The Christian Minister in India* (1946) by Charles Ranson, later General Secretary of the International Missionary Council, and *The Christian Minister in Africa* (1960) by Professor Sundkler of the University of Uppsala. And at last in 1958 the generous gift made available by Mr. Rockefeller through the Sealantic Fund, matched by comparable giving on the part of the great American missionary societies, is making possible advances that could hardly have been imagined twenty years ago.

The other point on which Tambaram 1938 laid special stress

[2] *The World Mission of the Church, Madras-Tambaram 1938* (London: International Missionary Council, 1939). p. 66.

was Christian literature. Millions of people all over the world are learning to read. The communists are well aware of the importance of capturing this market. They put money into it. Their material is attractively produced, adapted to the class of reader for whom it is intended, and produced at prices with which the ordinary publisher simply cannot compete. What are the churches doing? The answer must regrettably be that they are doing remarkably little. Specialists are few. It seems to be supposed that tired missionaries in their spare time and overworked younger church leaders will by some miracle produce admirable literature on every kind of topic. The list of Christian books in almost every language used by the younger churches is short enough to make an angel weep. Usually the I.M.C. does not take the initiative in setting new projects in hand; in this field it felt that an exception must be made:

> The ground on which the International Missionary Council believes that it must take the initiative in this matter is that most of the literature agencies on the field are either owned by, or financially dependent on literature societies, missions or churches of the sending countries. Until these bodies indicate a willingness to consider joint action in oversea work, plans for closer co-operation and, where necessary, unification of work on the field cannot be fully achieved.[3]

These were fine words. But, alas, they do things very slowly in the Christian world. The logical outcome of this affirmation should have been the setting up, by the I.M.C., of an international bureau of Christian literature. That is something for which in 1960 we still wait.

We met. We prayed. We talked. We departed. And in less than nine months we were once again at war. As so often in history some of the brightest hopes of Christian men and women were shattered on that hate and arrogance and cruelty that lie hidden in the depths of the human heart, and which only the power of the gospel of Christ can finally exorcise.

[3] *Ibid.*, p. 114.

IX

Dietrich Bonhoeffer and Worldly Christianity

"I SEEM TO GET MORE FROM THIS FELLOW BONHOEFFER THAN from anyone else." So said an American student, with that generous disregard of the right of foreigners to pronounce their languages in their own way, which is so characteristic of the Anglo-Saxon peoples. It was clear that this student had read *The Cost of Discipleship* many times and had been gripped by it as by no other theological work. In this there is something strange. When Dietrich Bonhoeffer died in 1945, he was almost unknown outside his own country, and even in Germany he did not rank among the most influential Christian thinkers. And now, more than ten years after his death, he seems to speak, as few others, with authority to a generation very different from his own.

It is always dangerous to generalise about generations. They change so rapidly, and there are always so many exceptions that no statement on the subject can have more than very limited validity. Yet remarks of teachers in many countries seem to indicate something like a common attitude among the young people of many countries today. After the war we were familiar with the cynical mood of many young men, who had fought for so much and gained so little. Then came the tortured idealism of the existentialists, trying to win some shred of hope out of despair. Now it seems as though we had entered into a mood of fairly serene contentment with a fairly serene world. "We are not interested in politics," say many of the young. "Our aim is to find a job, marry young, settle down, and enjoy bringing up a family in a community of like-minded and fairly honest people." When a speaker at a famous American College recently began his address with the words, "What are you prepared to die for?" he was met with looks of horrified and incredulous dismay. In a world where everything is relative, is there really anything worth dying for? Do not such phrases belong to the discredited mythology of the bad old men who made the wars?

But this is not true of all. There is no such mood in the communist countries, where the future still beckons in resplendent and fascinating colors. And some in the West are realising that the victory of the communists so far has lain in the spiritual and not in the material world. They have made the West profoundly uncertain of itself and suspicious of its own ideals. They have given the West a bad conscience—about imperialism and colonialism and a host of other things. If the West dies, it will be not through the shock of violent conflict, but through its own inner inanition; civilizations live only by the power of ideas and ideals, bitterly though these are derided by the hard-faced, practical men of both East and West. But what can we put before the young today? What will convince them that certain principles matter, that there are more important issues than having things as good as possible in a life that is bounded by the cares and duties of every day? It may be that Dietrich Bonhoeffer has the answer. The latest edition of the famous German theological encyclopedia *RGG* ascribes to him *"wegweisende Bedeutung,"* importance as a sign-post pointing to the future. Perhaps like Soren Kierkegaard he will come into his own only long after his death.

But we must go back in our story in order to put these things into their proper historical frame.

After the First World War the German people had been through a terrible time. Their glory had been laid in the dust. They were hungry, and the blockade was continued long after most people thought that it ought to have come to an end. The French occupied the Ruhr. The collapse of the German mark in 1923 wiped out, in a few days, the savings carefully stored up by many people over many years. There was no recovery and no hope. And then on January 30, 1933 Adolf Hitler came to power, by what methods of violence and chicanery it is not our purposes here to discuss. What was the German people to make of this new phenomenon?

Many accepted the new power with joy. It gave them work and hope and a sense of human dignity. Even in the German churches Hitler had his friends and spokesmen, men who were honestly convinced that in his rise and seizure of power they could see the hand of God at work in history. This comes out with strange intensity in some letters addressed by one distinguished theologian to another. The correspondents were Gerhard Kittel of Tuebingen and Karl Barth. "If I stand by the side of Christ," wrote Kittel, "I know nothing in the wide world—no sparrow on the roof-top, no lily in the field . . . no Palestinian zealots and no Roman Emperor, no Mussolini and no Hitler—in which the Almighty Creator of heaven and earth, who has revealed Himself to me as the Father of Jesus Christ, does not exercise His sovereign sway." A little later he goes on to state that a church that remained indifferent to what was taking place in the world, including what happened on January 30, 1933, would deny the authority and responsibility entrusted to it by the Lord of the church, who is at the same time the Lord of history. And then, in italics for emphasis, that "if the decision of world history in the life of a people lay between the Soviet star and the Germany of January 30th, the Church under God's Spirit and God's Word is not so poor as to lack full authority to say whether the decision of that day was from God or Satan." [1]

So here was a challenge clearly and firmly launched. A great many Christians in Germany at the time would have agreed completely with Kittel. This may seem strange in the light of all that we know today about Hitler and his monstrous regime. But the first art of the historical student is to project himself into the past and to see and feel things as the men of a past time saw and felt them, and in the light of the knowledge that they had in their own day. What did the average German know and feel in those years between 1933 and 1945?

"We didn't know." That is what most Germans will say today, and of course, there is hardly anyone in Germany who will admit that he ever was a Nazi. Naturally, there were many thousands of people in the know, as the regime developed the

[1] *Ein theologischer Briefwechsel,* pp. 10, 30, 34, quoted in *The Church and Its Function in Society, pp.* 226-27.

infamies of the Gestapo, of the massacre of the Jews and the liquidation of opponents. But the testimony of a large number of Germans of the deepest Christian conviction and sterling integrity cannot be disregarded. The average representative of a hard-working and rather unimaginative race, fully occupied in rebuilding his life and that of his family after the bad years, reading only a heavily censored press, and with few contacts outside Germany, had very little idea of what his government was up to. He probably knew that a few miles from his home there was a large area enclosed by electrified barbed wire, from which all strangers were strictly warned away. But everyone knew that there were unstable and disloyal elements in the nation, and that it was the business of the Fuehrer to take care of them. People in the East would become aware that the streets inhabited by Jews had become strangely silent. But movements of populations on a large scale had not been unknown in post-war Europe—had not a million Greeks been transferred from Asia Minor to mainland Greece in 1923?—and who in the world could have imagined that in the civilized twentieth century a maniac was planning the crime of the elimination of six million Jews? These things would be quite incredible, if they had not actually happened.

But there were some Germans who were more or less aware of what was going on, and they were faced by the darkest of uncertainties and the most difficult of decisions. For it was not a question simply of protesting against this crime or that. A fundamental principle was involved. How far can the claim of the state go? Patriotism is generally recognised as a virtue. The Bible bids us render to Caesar the things that are Caesar's. But what if Caesar begins to claim also the things that are God's? And where does the boundary lie between the two claims, and who is to determine it? For Hitler there was no problem; the state was to all intents and purposes God, and obedience to it was the highest duty of man. The church could be tolerated and protected just in so far as it lent itself to the purposes of the regime. But not all could see it in such simple terms as these, and there were no precedents from recent times to guide the critics.

The Church is clearly facing today one of the major crises of its history. It is confronted once again with a problem analogous to that which met it in its early days as it faced the Roman world. The question which arose then, and which meets us again today, is one which Professor Ernest Barker has described as perhaps the profoundest in history—the question of the relation between the Church as owning allegiance to a supra-mundane authority and the integrated body which is community-state or state-community.[2]

The surprising thing is not that so many Germans were perplexed and uncertain as that so many, and from so early a date, saw clearly the direction in which the new regime was carrying them and were prepared to say, if necessary at the cost of their lives, "Let the church be the church."

The "Confessing Church" came into existence. This phrase is strange in English and needs a word of explanation. It implies not the formation of a new and separate church, but the coming together of those within the German churches who were prepared to stand fast by the great Confessions of Faith of the period of the Reformation, with their affirmation of the sovereignty of Jesus Christ over church and world alike. It implies also a willingness to bear a good confession before the world to the truths of the gospel and of the great Christian traditions. In the period after 1933 it involved also a willingness to stand up to Hitler and his followers within the churches and to repudiate the exaggerated claims to obedience and loyalty that they were making. In May, 1934 the "Confessing Synod" of the German Evangelical Church met at Barmen. It put forth that famous Declaration which was as a beacon of light in a dark world:

Jesus Christ, as witness is borne to us concerning him in the Holy Scriptures, is the sole Word of God to which we must hearken, and which we must trust and obey, whether in life or in death.

We reject as false the doctrine that the Church can and should recognize, as sources for its proclamation, besides and

[2] *The Churches Survey Their Task*, pp. 9, 10.

apart from this sole Word of God, other events and powers, forms and truths as a revelation from God.[3]

"Whether in life or in death." It is easy to write such splendid words. Who would dare to assert, before the trial has been made, that he is capable of living them out? I have had in my own hands original documents from the files of the Gestapo, in which are to be found reports on every Protestant pastor and every Roman Catholic priest in a whole area. The Germans are a thorough people. A friend has described to me what it felt like to preach Sunday after Sunday, knowing well that at every service there was a spy in the congregation. It was not enough to be careful about what you said. What you did not say might be equally important, and failure to put in the right laudatory words about the regime, the duly fulsome prayers for "the great leader whom Thou, O God, hast given us," might land you in trouble with the authorities. This friend knew that it could only be a question of time. He was right. The fateful day came when the Gestapo arrived, and he was carried off to spend more than three years as Hitler's guest in Dachau, one of the worst of the concentration camps. This particular friend survived to emerge again, to be elected to high office in his Church, and to write an account of his experiences in which there is not a single trace of bitterness or hatred. There were many who disappeared and who never came out again; the record of all they endured and suffered is known to God only.

The man who attracted the greatest attention at this time, in Germany and outside it, was Martin Niemoeller. This remarkable man had served in the German Navy and at the close of the war in 1918 had been a submarine commander. Feeling the call to ordination, he had carried out the full course of theological studies, and in 1931 had been appointed pastor of Dahlem, a suburb of Berlin. Here his plain and courageous sermons attracted wide attention, and his voice was heard far beyond the limits of Germany. Such temerity could not but provoke the rulers. Niemoeller was actually acquitted by the

[3] Quoted in *A History of the Ecumenical Movement*, p. 466.

court which tried him. But he was far too dangerous a man to be at large; he was arrested again and confined as Hitler's personal prisoner—a new and strange category—in a succession of concentration camps from 1937 to 1945. During those years he had little to do but study the Bible, pray, and deepen his hold on the basic verities of the Christian faith. Since the war Niemoeller has served in a variety of great positions, and is a well-loved figure in half the countries of the world. But perhaps he has done more in silence than in speech; perhaps his greatest years were those in which he held on in loneliness and suffering, a symbol to the whole of the free world of the truth that loyalty to Jesus Christ must come before all other things, even before life itself.

The church has always had its martyrs, but now martyrdom had a new and special pain, referred to in moving terms by the Swedish bishop Johannes Sandegren at the Tambaram Conference in 1938. In the days of the Roman Empire, as for Savonarola in Florence in the fifteenth century and for the English martyrs under Queen Mary in England, death meant a public spectacle, with crowds of sorrowing friends and multitudes of perplexed and interested people. The testimony of last words and of a courageous death might exercise untold influence on the future. Now martyrdom would come obscurely in some unknown prison, perhaps accompanied by torture; bereaved families might receive much later a little casket of white dust. And the prisoners would be accompanied all the time by the nagging, agonizing doubt whether all this suffering was worth while. To suffer demands courage; to suffer and to hold on, although the suffering seems meaningless, is the work of supermen.

And so we come back to Dietrich Bonhoeffer. The outward facts of this short life can be briefly recorded. Bonhoeffer had served for a short time as pastor of a German church in Barcelona, had studied for a year at Union Theological Seminary, New York, and carried out a rather longer spell of pastoral service in London. He had thus a far wider knowledge of the world and of the churches outside Germany than almost any other German churchman of his time. When the second war started in 1939, he was in America and could have stayed there; he felt that God wanted him to be in Germany, and so he returned. From a very early date he had been occupied with the affairs of the Confessing Church, and had come under the suspicion of the government. Permission to teach, to speak, to write, to live in Berlin had gradually been withdrawn from him. In 1942 Bonhoeffer made an astonishing journey to Stockholm, in order to meet Dr. Bell, the Bishop of Chichester, and other leaders in the world church. He convinced Bell of the range and importance of the opposition to Hitler in Germany; unfortunately, Bell's representations to the British government, as was perhaps to be expected in the middle of a great war, did not meet with much attention. Things could not go on like this; it was hardly a surprise to Bonhoeffer's friends when news came that on April 5, 1943 he had been arrested by the Gestapo. For eighteen months after his arrest he was able to carry on a somewhat extensive, though clandestine, correspondence with his friends. Then came the grave shock of the failure of the attempt on the life of Hitler in 1944. Bonhoeffer's brother and two of his brothers-in-law were taken and executed. Many friends hoped that he might be spared, but it was not to be. Just at the end of the war, in the crisis of the debacle of Hitler's power, Dietrich Bonhoeffer was hanged in prison by the Nazis.

What was the secret of his power? To one who did not know him personally it seems that he was one of those fortunate persons born with a genius for friendship. All kinds of people—churchmen, students, working men, atheists—seem to have been drawn to him and to have found in him a sincerity, a reality of inward life, which is often lacking in the professed and professional servants of the church. And from his published works it is clear that until the last day of his life he was always learning, always finding fresh things in Jesus Christ.

He was not a ready writer. With much of the poet in his make up he could see visions and dream dreams, but the labor of getting his thoughts down in black and white on paper in systematic form was heavy. Among his papers are various outlines of the books that he was going to write, but most of these books remained unwritten. His influence in the world today is due to a few shorter works that were completed, to the fragmentary and uncompleted *Ethics,* above all to the *Letters and Papers from Prison* that were gathered and edited by a friend after his death.

The early pages of the *Ethics* reveal the intensity of the blow that had been struck by Hitler at all conventional Christianity. What do we mean by ethics? All the old formulations seem to be meaningless in face of a world in which all values have been transformed, in which the devil seems to have taken on the form of an angel of light, and draws near to the Christian with alluring invitations couched in terms that used to stand for righteousness. One man believes that he can face this need in terms of conscience. But how can he trust his individual conscience when the whole flow of the world's events seems to be moving against it? Another speaks of duty. But what is a man to do when basic duties seem to be in conflict with one another? Another withdraws from the turmoil of life to develop the ideal of a purely inner saintliness and devotion to Christ. But such a man can have no influence at all on the course of events. And is he in truth following the man of Nazareth, who was always about the streets and lanes of Galilee, and ended his days on a Cross?

So Bonhoeffer is driven back, amid the shifts and whirls of modern life, to the one place where a rock is to be found. Jesus Christ is a reality. He lived; in the pages of the Gospels we can see what God is and what goodness is. Ethics is not a science that can be reduced to formulae and equations. It is the desperate venturing of a man upon decisions for which there is no chart or clue, in trust and hope that God will not forsake him, and that Jesus Christ will manifest himself as the unchanging reality:

O wondrous change! Those hands once so strong and active, have now been bound. Helpless and forlorn, you see the end of your deed. Yet with a sigh of relief you resign your cause to a stronger hand, and are content to do so. For one brief moment you enjoyed the bliss of freedom, only to give it back to God, that he might perfect it in glory.[4]

[4] *Letters and Papers from Prison* (London: S. C. M. Press, 1953), p. 170.

The *Ethics* remain a noble fragment, only a small part of what Bonhoeffer might have given us. It is perhaps in the *Letters and Papers from Prison* that the ordinary reader will feel that he can come close to one of the most remarkable Christians of our time. In the concentration camp Bonhoeffer had to share the life of ordinary men, all sorts of men, as he had never shared it before. He became increasingly aware of the appalling distance that separates the churches and their members from the way in which ordinary men think and live their lives and make their decisions. And almost to his surprise he found that he liked these ordinary men very much. They seemed so real, and so much that goes on in the churches seemed by comparison to fall under the condemnation of a pale and unproductive pietism. And so Bonhoeffer began to work out a new, and at first sight paradoxical, doctrine of the *worldliness* of the Christian faith. "The world" had been a negative force from which good Christians tended to shrink back in anxiety, if not in horror; now "the world" is to be one of the categories in which the Christian faith is to be re-expressed.

Only a rather long quotation can give the feel of this new direction in which Bonhoeffer's mind was moving:

During the last year or so I have come to appreciate the "worldliness" of Christianity as never before. The Christian is not a *homo religiosus,* but a man, pure and simple, just as Jesus was a man, compared with John the Baptist anyhow. I don't mean the shallow this-worldliness of the enlightened, of the busy, the comfortable or the lascivious. It's something much more profound than that, something in which the knowledge of death and resurrection is ever present. . . .

Later I discovered and am still discovering up to this very moment that it is only by living completely in the world that one learns to believe. . . . This is what I mean by worldliness—taking life in one's stride, with all its duties and its problems, its successes and failures, its experience and helplessness. It is in such a life that we throw ourselves utterly in the arms of God and participate in his sufferings in the world and watch with Christ in Gethsemane. That is faith, that is *metanoia,* and that is what makes a man and a Christian (cf. Jeremiah 45). How can success make us arrogant or failure lead us astray, when we participate in the sufferings of God by living in this world?[5]

We are fortunate in having from an eyewitness a description of Bonhoeffer's last days and hours. Payne Best, a captured British officer, writes:

Bonhoeffer was all humility and sweetness, he always seemed to me to diffuse an atmosphere of happiness, of joy in every smallest event in life, and of deep gratitude for the mere fact that he was alive. . . . He was one of the very few men that I have ever met to whom his God was real and close to him. . . . The following day, Sunday 8th April, 1945, Pastor Bonhoeffer held a little service and spoke to us in a manner which reached the hearts of all, finding just the right word to express the spirit of our imprisonment and the thoughts and resolutions which it had brought. He had hardly finished his last prayer when the door opened and two evil-looking men in civilian clothes came in and said: "Prisoner Bonhoeffer, get ready to come with us." Those words "come with us"—for all prisoners they had come to mean one thing only—the scaffold. We bade him goodbye—he drew me aside—"This is the end," he said, "for me the beginning of life," and then he gave me a message to give, if I could, to the Bishop of Chichester. . . . Next day at Flossenburg he was hanged.[6]

How strangely different life is from men's calculations! Hitler had affirmed that he was settling the future of Europe for a thousand years. To those who without warning heard on the radio the appalling news of Hitler's pact with Russia in 1939, it seemed for a moment that he might be speaking the truth. And yet within twelve years Hitler's Reich had gone down in unimaginable shame and disaster. And the church of Jesus Christ has proved itself once more one of those anvils that has worn out many hammers. "My shade's so much more potent than your flesh," said Browning's Bishop Blougram. It seems that he was right. To all appearances force is the mighty thing, and victory will always be on the side of the big

[5] *Letters and Papers from Prison,* pp. 168-69.
[6] *The Venlo Incident,* p. 180, quoted in *Letters and Papers,* pp. 11, 12.

battalions. But there is a disturbing story about a man named Jesus who was put on a cross and died, and yet is named with reverence and adoration in a million churches today across the world. Was he right after all, and was Pilate wrong? These men believed and sealed their testimony with their lives. Their name liveth for evermore.

We all say, "It couldn't happen here"—which is exactly what the Germans said before 1933. We now know that it could happen anywhere and at any time. If it did happen here, where would you and I stand?

X

D. T. Niles and the Future of Missions

On a steamy evening in the summer of 1927 four men sat on a verandah of the splendid Y.M.C.A. building in Colombo and talked. One was a young missionary recently out from Britain; one a Burgher, of the mixed race springing from Dutch and Ceylonese origins; one a Sinhalese-speaking Christian of the majority race in Ceylon; one a Tamil-speaking student of the University College of Colombo, who hailed from Jaffna in the extreme north of Ceylon. Another of the fated men of the ecumenical movement has entered on our scene.

Jaffna is a strange part of the world. Most of the inhabitants of Ceylon are Buddhists and speak Sinhalese. But more than a thousand years ago a number of Tamil-speaking Indians came in and settled in this northern and isolated corner of the island. They are very different from the race of hardy Indian laborers who, at a much later date, have come in to work on the tea and rubber estates of Ceylon, and present the Ceylon government with one of its most difficult problems. The Jaffna Tamils speak what they claim to be the purest Tamil in the world. The level of education and culture is very high. Here Daniel Thambiraja Niles was born in 1908, the son of a lawyer whose habit it was to read right through the Bible and the works of Shakespeare every year to keep up his knowledge of his religion and his understanding of human nature.

D. T., as he is generally known in the ecumenical world, early heard the call to ordination. A brilliant career at the Union Theological College, Bangalore, the best centre of theological teaching in Asia, brought him into touch with the latest movements of Western theological thought. A meeting with Visser 't Hooft at a quadrennial conference of the Indian Student Christian Movement left a deep impression on him. Travel in the West to attend other student conferences broadened his mind and his understanding of countries and churches other than his own.

Ten years passed. At the Tambaram Conference of 1938 a group of highly distinguished men and women were sitting round a table, trying to hammer out the Tambaram statement on the Christian faith—Henry Van Dusen, Georgia Harkness, Herbert Farmer of Cambridge, Hendrik Kraemer, and others. And there, almost inevitably, was D. T. Niles, perhaps at that time feeling a little overwhelmed at finding himself in such eminent company.

Another ten years passed. The First Assembly of the World Council of Churches was meeting for its opening service. Archbishops and moderators, cabinet ministers and professors, and the rest of them had with some difficulty been shepherded into their places. And then came the moment for the addresses. There were to be two, the first naturally by John R. Mott. The patriarch and prophet, already more than eighty years old, began to reminisce; there passed before his mind the figures of those great ones of the past with whom he had worked, who had served the ecumenical movement in their day, and then passed on into the unseen. It was perhaps inevitable that he should dwell a little in the past. Then the slim pastor of the Methodist Church of Ceylon, simply clad in the white robe of his people and looking younger than his forty years, stood up to speak. This was an address almost wholly directed to the future—strong, challenging, and consoling. God has bidden Moses go down and speak to Pharaoh. But who is Moses that he should make his way into the presence of the king, and what assurance is there that Pharaoh will listen? God has bidden us go to the world with a message concerning his Son. But who are we that we should go? Do we even know what it is that we have to say? But our confidence is not in ourselves. The everlasting God is one who never changes, and it is he who has bidden us go forward.

Ten more years have brought fresh honors—an honorary doctor's degree, the chairmanship of the World's Student Christian Federation and the launching of a great four-year venture of study on the Mission of the Church in the world, and finally the secretaryship of the East Asia Christian Conference. Truly the younger churches have arrived with a vengeance!

As we saw, from Tambaram 1938 onwards the equality of the younger and older churches was no longer a subject of debate. It had been accepted in principle and with enthusiasm by all the older churches. This did not mean, however, that all problems had been solved; there were still adjustments to be made and possible sources of tension that had to be faced. It was to some of these problems that the Whitby Missionary Conference of 1947 directed its attention.

Whitby, Ontario, is a quiet little town. The Conference that met there in July 1947, the first gathering of the scattered missionary forces after the end of the war, was small and hard-working. It produced a number of brilliant reports and one brilliant phrase, "Partnership in Obedience." It is a matter for great regret that Whitby and its reports have never been taken very seriously in the Christian world. Preparations for Amsterdam 1948 were already well on the way when it met; the larger conference overshadowed the smaller, and Whitby's prophetic utterances fell for the most part on deaf ears. It is time that the churches went back and picked up the threads that have been dropped.

What Whitby was concerned about was the appalling fact that in the middle of the twentieth century nearly half the people living in the world have never even heard the name of Jesus Christ. Sixty years earlier John R. Mott had electrified the churches by his famous slogan, "The evangelization of the world in this generation." You cannot put life into a phrase that has had its day and no longer rings bells in the minds of the hearers. Yet the problem still remains. In the Ascension the lordship of Jesus over heaven and earth has been proclaimed and ratified. But in Tibet the lordship of Jesus is not even denied; the inhabitants do not know enough about it even to deny it.

At eventide King Jesus
Lay down in Joseph's grave;
The peoples were untroubled
Whom Jesus died to save.

What was true on the first Good Friday is still largely true today; the peoples are untroubled by the gospel because they have never heard it.

The problem of 1947 is in the main the same as the problem of 1887. But one immense change has taken place, in the intervening years, in the formulation of the problem. In 1887, in countless areas of the world the church just did not exist; if it was to come into existence at all, this could only be by a Western invasion in the name of Christ. But now in almost every part of the world a church exists. These younger churches are charged with the task of the total evangelization of their countries. The gospel must be preached to every creature. But in this new setting of the task what are the respective parts to be played by older and younger churches? It would be quite easy to say that there is no problem. The younger churches might say to the older, and have sometimes been inclined to say, "Thank you very much; you have started this, and now we will carry on. You can all go home." But this simple isolationism is really a form of heresy. The older churches equally might say to the younger, "We are very busy here; we have the gigantic task of post-war reconstruction; we are faced with the problems of communism and the reconstruction of our whole way of thinking. We can no longer spare you even the minimal resources that we have given you in the past. We will now stay at home." But this too would be heresy, though of a rather different kind.

Whitby found the answer in the new formula of "Partnership in Obedience." Each word in the phrase is significant. Older and younger churches alike are faced with a new situation, which demands a new kind of obedience. Each must work out in independence the nature of that obedience. But as they do so, they will find themselves partners, because older and younger alike are trying to discover the will of a common Lord. Oddly enough, D. T. Niles was not at Whitby in 1947, but no younger church leader has drunk more deeply of its spirit.

In the following year a first step was taken to implement some of the Whitby ideas. The first East Asia Conference was convened in Manila, jointly by the World Council (in process of formation) and the International Missionary Council. This was a strange and moving meeting. Only two foreigners were present; all the other members were leaders in the East Asian churches. Yet hardly any of these men had ever met one another before. Here we meet the part tragic, part comic situation produced by the follies of Western missions. Our missions have been like the spokes of a wheel; they all run in to centers in Europe or America, but no thought at all had been given to creating contact and fellowship round the rim. Thus, hundreds of Indonesian students had crossed the world to study in Holland, but although Australia and Indonesia almost touch not a single Indonesian had ever been at an Australian university. The Indian Student Christian Federation had sent students to conferences in Indonesia, but the ordinary churchman in India was hardly aware that churches even existed in Indonesia. So it was a great day for these Asians, when for the first time they met as Asians, and for no other purpose than to consider the greater good of the churches in East Asia. Their first thought was that they would have no difficulty in agreeing. It was something of a shock to them to discover that they tended to disagree with one another more sharply than with their friends from the West, and that it was sometimes the foreigner who had to serve as catalyst and interpreter.

This exciting conference led to one notable result—the setting up, once again jointly by the W.C.C. and the I.M.C., of the East Asia Secretariat. At first the churches were not at all sure that they wanted such an office. Might this not lead to their being fobbed off with a local and second-rate form of ecumenism, instead of having direct access, like other churches, to the centers of ecumenical activity? It was only when it was carefully explained to them that the existence of the Secretariat would in no way jeopardise these direct contacts that they were prepared to be convinced of its usefulness. Much depended on the choice of the first secretary. He must be a man of great tact and sensitiveness, able to help the churches toward mutual understanding and fellowship, without in the least giving the impression that he was there to direct or to enforce instructions given from without. After careful thought the post was offered to Rajah B. Manickam, who after a period of study in

America had served with distinction as General Secretary of the National Christian Council of India. The choice was good. Manickam served the churches well and did exactly what was wanted; he made separated churches aware of one another and helped them forward in the path of fellowship and responsibility. He left the office in 1956 to become bishop of Tranquebar, the first Indian bishop of the Lutheran Churches in India.

One of the two foreigners present at the Manila Conference had been so stirred by these events that he wrote in to the ecumenical headquarters to suggest that this was a pattern that might well be followed elsewhere, and that the time had come to divide the world into eight regions—North America, Europe, the Muslim world, the Orthodox churches, Africa south of the Sahara, East Asia, the South Pacific, and Latin America. It had not been found possible for the W.C.C. and the I.M.C. to combine at the center; on the circumference they had found it possible to work in harmony, and the development of such co-operation would be the surest method of bringing them together in the end. No notice was taken at the time of this highly imaginative proposal, but in a strange way the history of the last ten years has tended to turn imagination into fact.

First we must take note of another "ecumenical" movement which had begun to manifest itself in East Asia. This took its origin in the Philippines, that country so different from any other in the world, which, though Protestant missions there have a history of little more than sixty years, has produced some of the outstanding leadership in the Christian world and a vigorous sense of national independence which is prepared to assert itself against all comers. This movement was primarily concerned with interchurch aid and exchange of personnel between the churches of East Asia. The name "ecumenical" had been adopted without any consultation with either of the main ecumenical bodies, and though this is not a patented and trademark term, there was a certain amount of natural irritation in high quarters. Such division could not be allowed to go on; all the forces working for unity and mutual understanding must be brought closer together. Somewhat delicate negotiations followed; the result of them was the East Asia Christian Conference, held in March 1957 at Prapat in Sumatra under the chairmanship of Bishop Sobrepena of the United Church of Christ in the Philippines.

By this time the reader of these chapters may be inclined to say, "What, another conference?" And indeed there are far too many conferences that are just conferences, opportunities for people to get together and talk. Of such no notice whatever has been taken in this book. But at Prapat something genuinely new came into being. There had previously been Christian conferences in Asian lands, but almost without exception these had been planned and organized by Christians from the West, and the Asians had found themselves really in the position of guests in their own country. Prapat was genuinely a conference of the Asian churches. It had been planned and arranged by them. Chairman and vice-chairman and most of the official delegates were Asians. Representatives from many other countries were there and were welcomed, but this time unmistakably it was they who were the guests. In a new way the Asian churches had come into their own.

Prapat did two important things. It organized the East Asia Christian Conference as a permanent body, with D. T. Niles as secretary and Kyaw Than of Burma, a former secretary of the Student Federation in Geneva, as assistant secretary. And by appointing a New Zealander, Alan Brash, as its secretary for interchurch aid, the Conference indicated both its entire freedom from race or color prejudice and also its sense of the new relationship in which the English-speaking dominions of the South Pacific stand to the world of Asia. For more than a century Australia, in spite of its proximity to Asia and its fears of possible Japanese aggression, had turned its face the other way, historically to Britain and economically to the United States. But now the war and the logic of history had brought about a change; Australia and New Zealand must recognize that they have a special responsibility, as nominally Christian countries, in relation to that great continent in which are to be found half of the inhabitants of the world. It was symbolic of the change that the urgent needs of the rapidly growing church of Timor in Indonesia should have been met by the sending of missionaries from Australia.

The East Asia Conference has met again (at Kuala Lumpur

in 1959). But perhaps more significant for our present purpose was the meeting of the first All-Africa Christian Conference in January 1958. When the delegates arrived at Ibadan in Nigeria, the greatest purely African city in the world, they must have been almost compelled to say in wonder, "What hath God wrought." In Asia, after all, missions have gone on for centuries and most of the inhabitants of the Philippines have been Christians at least in name for four hundred years. But here everything is so new. A century ago when Livingstone, fresh from the first of his great African journeys, begged leave to draw the attention of the University of Cambridge to Africa, over the whole heart of the continent was written the single word "unexplored." There were little Christian settlements on the coast; in the interior a man could travel literally thousands of miles and never encounter any evidence that Jesus had ever lived and died. And now these Africans had come from every territory in Africa, with the single exception of the small Spanish colonies, as the representatives of great and growing churches. No one knows how many Christians there are in Africa. Certainly there are more than there were in the Roman Empire when Constantine made Christianity the official religion of the Empire. In Eastern Nigeria it is reckoned that 48 per cent of the population is Christian. The Kabaka of Buganda, grandson of the persecuting king of seventy years ago, rules over a million and a half Africans, of whom considerably more than half are now at least in name members of the Roman Catholic or the Anglican Church.

The Conference was not without its problems. White South Africans born in Africa claim that they too are Africans, a claim that the black Africans are not always ready to admit. There were moments of tension between representatives of the Dutch Church in South Africa, which is committed to the doctrine of *apartheid,* and other Africans to whom *apartheid* is as the sin of witchcraft. The Conference was presided over, with dignity and charm, by a distinguished Nigerian, Sir Francis Ibiam, and was received by the Prime Minister of Western Nigeria, Chief Awolowo, a sincere and practising Methodist. But it was recognised that, though the vast majority of educated Africans are in some sense Christians, a large number of the leaders are no longer practising members of any church. African independence is going ahead apace. In the brief period since the conference met, tremendous changes have taken place in the French union, leading to far greater African autonomy. Even in the Belgian Congo the tide is coming in, and Africans who had been content with colonial status are demanding something else. Who is going to take the lead? The thoughtful African finds himself torn in three—by the claims of the ancient African traditions of his people, by the demands of the gospel that he learned in Sunday school, and by the exciting modern pull of secularism, with or without a communist handhold on the rope.

The Conference was not very well organised. But the important thing about it was that it happened, and that it planned to give itself permanence. A continuing committee was appointed, with a secretary, and the mandate to prepare for another conference in about three years' time. It is clear that Africa south of the Sahara is well on the way to constituting itself a "region," in the sense in which the term was used above.

In 1960 or 1961 an All Latin American Conference is due to take place. The vigorous independence and individualism of Latin American Evangelical Christians is such that it is never certain whether they can be persuaded to co-operate about anything. But here is another area in which the formation of a "region" is overdue, and in which, for the first time, it has been made possible, through the yeoman service of the D C-3 airplane, that modern packhorse of the vast stretches of the Pampas and of the hidden valleys of the Andes. Also in 1961 we look forward to the holding of a conference for the South Pacific, that generally neglected region of the world, the most extensive of all, if we count the broad stretches of the Pacific, the smallest in terms of actual land surface and population, yet with a noble record of Christian service and of martyrdom for the sake of the faith. One of the greatest needs of this area is a united theological school for the higher training of its ministers; at present there seems to be literally no body or authority through which such a school could come into being.

It is perhaps not without interest that the churches of the

European continent have found it desirable to hold a meeting on their own. Early in 1959 they met in Denmark, like others gave themselves a permanent organization, and elected as their secretary H. H. Harms, at that time a distinguished member of the staff of the World Council of Churches in Geneva. It really looks as though the regional organization was something that had come to stay.

But these are outward things. The inner problems of readjustment are much more subtle and must occupy us for a little time. In this new world what, if any, is the relationship of the missionary from the West to these new and proudly independent younger churches?

In the last fifty years an immense amount has been done to transfer the leadership from Western to Asian and African hands. There was a touching illustration of this at the Lambeth Conference of Anglican bishops in 1948. For the first time the delegation of Chinese bishops was led by a Chinese presiding bishop, Lindel Tsen of Honan. He was accompanied by his Canadian assistant, Bishop W. C. White. But many years before, when Bishop White was diocesan bishop of Honan, Lindel Tsen had been consecrated to be his assistant. Now in his old age the Canadian was joyfully serving as assistant to the Chinese who had earlier been his own assistant.

Much has been done to transfer property and financial responsibility to the younger churches. In the past a great deal of valuable property had been held by "the mission," and in consequence the local church had felt little interest either in the property or in the use to which it was put. Now it has been almost universally recognized that the church is the body which matters—the mission as such must gradually disappear.

But the problem of the relation of the missionary to the church still remains. It has to be recognised that the words "mission" and "missionary" are very much disliked by most of the younger churches. They speak of a period of alien domination, and particularly of a period of Western financial control, in which, although independence might have been given in name to the younger church, the financial dominance exercised from London or New York in fact made it impossible for it to act on its own initiative or in accordance with its own desires. Some great churches have now abandoned the term "missionary" and replaced it by the term "fraternal worker." For this there is a good deal to be said; the new term has a suggestion of equality and informality that was lacking in the old. And the change in words is meant to correspond to a real change in thought. Now the church in the field is to be the free and indigenous expression of the Christian faith; the foreigner is there just to serve the church as it may desire.

So far so good. But we have not yet answered our question. Is the fraternal worker a member and minister of the church which he serves, or is he not? In the past missionaries have sometimes retained their official membership in their home church and have never transferred it to the church which they served in Asia or Africa. Will the fraternal worker do the same? And if so is this a sound and correct relationship? Where, as has sometimes happened, the local church has been organised on racial or national lines, it seems impossible for a foreigner to become a member of it, unless he changes his nationality at the same time. Recently, when a young German went out to Indonesia to serve an independent younger church, the missionary society which sent him out had not even considered the question of his relation to the church that he was to serve. It had not even occurred to them that there was a problem. He was a missionary, a being of a special and particular kind and class; he would not need to have anything to do with the church, and the church would have no direct responsibility for him. In some cases the foreign worker, being unable to work within the church and not wishing to set up a parallel organization outside it, has been reduced to a state of total paralysis and frustration, and has wondered whether he really made a mistake when he crossed half the world to preach Christ to those who have not heard of him.

Clearly we are in a state of considerable confusion. The relation of missionary to national seems to have passed through three phases. In the first the missionary was feared and loved and respected. He represented authority, the authority of a father over his children. Then came the time when the missionary was disliked and criticized. The younger church leader claimed freedom and felt that the missionary was holding on far too long to a purely artificial situation of control. Now comes the time when the foreigner is regarded with indifference. The younger church leaders know that control is in their own hands. They do not really mind very much whether the foreigner is there or not; the question no longer interests them.

"Personally, I prefer the term missionary." The speaker was D. T. Niles, the date September 9, 1959.

Two days before this chapter was written, an unexpected meeting took place in Geneva between the subject of this chapter and the writer of it. The main theme of a long conversation was precisely that of the chapter. Why has the message of Whitby never been heard, and what can we do to make sure that it is heard? Some years ago Niles scandalized the general secretary of a great missionary society by asking for more missionaries for Ceylon. When asked why in the world he suggested that missionaries were needed by what is probably the best educated and most advanced younger church in the world, he replied succinctly, "to finish the unfinished task." In 1958 the general secretary of the Indian Student Christian Movement startled his British friends, and gravely perplexed a number of his Asian friends, by suggesting that the West should send out a number of missionaries for special work among the students of India. Are we passing out of the third phase?

That is what Whitby 1947 was trying to say. There is a gigantic unfinished task before us. All the resources of all the churches together are quite inadequate to finish it in our day and generation. Can we get together, on a basis of intelligent planning and loyal co-operation, to see who can and should do what before it is too late? In face of this task, in its modern dimension, the old distinctions between East and West, older and younger, missionary and national fade into insignificance, as each tries to be obedient to the Lord of the harvest and loyal to his colleague in the harvest field.

One of the very few younger church leaders who has seen this new vision of the unfinished task is D. T. Niles. Another is his assistant secretary Kyaw Than. Is it possible that these are the forerunners of a new generation of younger church leadership, qualified to present to the West a call to service and self-sacrifice which the West will neglect at its peril?

XI

At Last: The World Council of Churches

IN THE COURSE OF THIS STUDY WE HAVE ENCOUNTERED A NUMBER of men who seem, from the day of their birth, to have been predestined to take part in ecumenical affairs. One was G. K. A. Bell, the Bishop of Chichester, another J. H. Oldham. We have still to make the acquaintance of two others in the same tradition, though very distinct in character and outlook from the older men.

At Stockholm 1925 the youngest member of the Conference was a Dutchman named Willem Adolf Visser 't Hooft, who had shortly before taken up work with the Y.M.C.A. We have already seen that in 1937 Visser 't Hooft had been chosen to co-operate with Oldham in writing the preparatory book for the Oxford Conference, *The Church and Its Place in Society.* At Tambaram 1938 one of the younger delegates, who knew Visser 't Hooft well by reputation and had expected to meet a bearded veteran of the vintage of Oldham, or at least of William Paton, was astonished to find that the slim young Dutchman sitting next him was none other than the already famous Church leader, and that he was in fact no more than a few months his senior in age.

When the Provisional Committee, charged with the task of bringing a World Council of Churches into being, met at Utrecht in May, 1938, there was no doubt at all as to who should be chairman. As we have seen, William Temple was unanimously chosen as of all men then living the best fitted for this post. There was far less agreement in the choice of a general secretary. Visser 't Hooft's name had been put forward and had met with a good deal of approval. Some, however, felt that at thirty-seven a man was too young for so gigantic a task. It was Temple's authority which turned the scale; the young general secretary of the World's Student Christian Federation was chosen. William Paton of Britain and Henry Smith Leiper of the United States were asked to share with him his formidable responsibilities.

Looking back over twenty-one years, it is possible to doubt whether any better choice could have been made.

Visser 't Hooft ("Wim" to friends of later years, "Mouse" to Dutch friends of earlier years) starts, like Nathan Soederblom, with the great advantage of ready utterance in four languages—Dutch, English, German, and French—and the ability to read several others. In his years with the Student Federation he had traveled widely, and with alert observation had made himself familiar with the conditions and the problems of many churches. In those years his sensitiveness to currents of thought, his willingness to try out new experiments and to abandon methods of work that were no longer relevant were proverbial. In all these years of rapid movement from conference to conference, and of intervals of office work surrounded by the dismal files that seem inseparable from ecumenical activity, 't Hooft has never lost his intellectual interests and has an acquaintance with modern theological literature, mainly German, such as many professors of theology might envy. A brilliant mind, more effective in analysis than in construction, enables him to go quickly to the heart of almost any situation. By his quickness of thought he can dominate almost any committee. On the platform his speech is almost always effective, sometimes profoundly moving. He has in very high degree the capacity to win and to hold the confidence of older men and to win and to hold the admiration of younger men. Beneath all these many qualifications lies a quiet and resolute faith in Jesus Christ, so restrained in expression that casual observers might well fail to realise what is the driving force behind everything that the man does.

In twenty years the World Council of Churches has come to be deeply marked by its first general secretary, both in his strength and in his limitations.

Every great man has his limitations. For instance in early years 't Hooft came deeply under the influence of Karl Barth and his theology. Some have felt that this has made him less sympathetic than he might have been with points of view other than those of continental theology. The gravest limitation, however, has been that the general secretary of the World Council of Churches is not and never has been a churchman in the professional sense of that term. Although an ordained pastor of his church, the Dutch Reformed Church, he has never held a parish and has not that knowledge, which only experience can give, of the life of the church as it is lived out at "the grass-roots" of parish and community. One of the criticisms of the World Council that has most frequently been heard is that it is simply the World's Student Christian Federation grown up—a criticism which, as the years have passed, has had less and less basis in reality.

We must go back to 1938. Hardly had the Provisional Committee of the World Council of Churches begun its work, when the Second World War burst on the world. Plans to hold the first Assembly in 1941 had to be given up at once. It seemed as though the war years might be years of total loss as far as ecumenical advance was concerned. Once again history has confounded expectation; in point of fact those years of distress were perhaps the most creative years in the whole process of ecumenical development.

In the first place, just because those united in the faith were so deeply separated from one another by the catastrophes of human folly, there was a deeper sense of spiritual awareness and mutual concern. All this was summed up in the noble words of Bishop Berggrav of Oslo, written in 1945 just after the war had ended: "In these last years we have lived more intimately with each other than in times when we could communicate with each other. We have prayed together more, we listened together more to the Word of God, our hearts were together more."

But there were also directly practical services to be carried out. Until the final occupation of the whole of France by the Germans in 1942, some measure of contact could be maintained; Visser 't Hooft was able to travel to Britain as late as the spring of 1942. But when all visible contacts were cut off, the real work began. Since Switzerland was neutral, there were Germans in Geneva and on the staff of the World Council of Churches. The general secretary had contacts in all countries, and by devious and sometimes dangerous methods information continued to flow into the World Council's office from many isolated places. The Nazis were not unaware of this. A secret Gestapo document published after the war states that the influence of the ecumenical movement on German church life is considerable, and orders that a Nazi agent is to be infiltrated into the ecumenical bodies in Geneva. It is believed that this order was never carried out. Certainly no member of the devoted and overworked staff looked in the least like a Nazi agent, but presumably the last thing a Nazi agent would look like would be a Nazi agent![1]

During these years a strange, and as it has turned out, permanent transformation came about. Ecumenical movements had been means to enable people to talk to one another; they had had little occasion to engage in anything very practical. Now, driven by the necessity of the times, the World Council became fully operational.

The first area of need to attract the attention of the staff was that of prisoners of war. The Red Cross, as ever, rendered splendid service in helping to meet the physical needs of prisoners. To some extent the World Council was able to help with spiritual ministrations to thousands of isolated men and women, who discovered, perhaps for the first time, that the world-wide fellowship of the children of Christ is something more than a pious dream.

Next came the refugees. Countless individuals and families were being uprooted from their homes. Much experience had been gathered during the First World War, and in the interval between the wars, of problems of this kind. The World Council was the natural clearing house for those in different countries who were trying to alleviate the extreme misery of the displaced and the homeless. When the war ended, it was thought that these efforts would have to be continued for perhaps five years. It was not foreseen that fifteen years after the end of the war this problem would still be with us, and that as soon as needs in one area had been to some extent met, tragedy would at once break out in some new area. The World Council's division of aid to refugees is still one of the most active parts of the whole organization.

[1] See *A History of the Ecumenical Movement,* p. 710.

The war had brought to many countries destruction on a scale unparalleled since the Thirty Years' War three centuries before. It was clear that whole peoples would be cold and hungry and homeless, and that the churches in the devastated countries would have the utmost difficulty in rebuilding their shattered work. As early as 1942 plans were put in hand for the work of reconstruction and interchurch aid. So carefully had these plans been laid that, as each area was liberated, the department was able to move in and to begin its beneficent work. Before long countries such as Holland and Norway, which had been receiving countries, began to be sending countries. The greater part of the gifts came from the United States, but almost every country in the world seemed to be eager to co-operate. It is important not to forget the services rendered by governments and by Roman Catholic and Jewish agencies. But it is no exaggeration to say that in the whole history of the Christian churches there has never been so great, so sustained, and so simply generous a manifestation of Christian charity as this.

At last the war ended. Christians were able to look at one another once more and to ask what the next steps should be in taking up the work of building that had been begun. The first anxiety was as to relationships between those who had been, as far as political loyalties were concerned, enemies during the war. This time there was no need for anxiety. When a World Council group went to Stuttgart in October 1945 to meet a number of German church leaders, these leaders made a declaration in which they fully recognised their participation in the guilt of the German people and expressed their desire again to share fully in the work of ecumenical development. In later times these German churchmen have had to face rather sharp criticism from their own side; it has been felt that they laid down their arms too easily and accepted too meekly the judgment of the outside world on what had happened in Germany since 1933. The immediate effect, however, was splendid. The question of "war guilt," which had so long bedevilled ecumenical relationships after the first war, this time simply did not arise. German after German has declared that in those days of renewal only in church circles could Germans feel that they were at once accepted and trusted as colleagues and brethren.

One of the first questions, naturally, was that of the first Assembly of the World Council, still in process of formation. The first post-war meeting of the Provisional Committee was held at Geneva in February 1946. As we have seen, it takes three full years to prepare adequately for an international conference. But already five years had passed since the date originally fixed for the Assembly. Fifty churches had signified their desire to join the World Council, in addition to the fifty which had been committed before the war started. People were getting impatient. Urgent pleas that the Assembly should not be held before 1949 were overruled, and it was decided that the meeting should take place in August 1948. This means that the preparations were far less thorough than those for Edinburgh 1910 and for Oxford 1937. And some were not happy about the choice of Amsterdam as the place of meeting. The International Missionary Council has usually chosen quiet places for its meetings. A great city, especially when that city is crowded with visitors and absorbed in preparations for the inauguration of a new Queen, is hardly a restful backcloth for profound theological cogitations. Yet so the decision was made, and so it was carried out.

In August, 1948 the representatives of more than a hundred churches came together in the Concertgebouw at Amsterdam. Their first task was to decide whether there should be a World Council at all, whether its provisional status as "in process of formation" should be exchanged for a real and official existence. On the morning of August 23 a greatly honored representative of the French Protestant Church, Marc Boegner, rose and proposed formally: "That the first Assembly of the World Council of Churches be declared to be and is hereby constituted . . . and that the formation of the World Council of Churches be declared to be and is hereby completed." The chairman, Geoffrey Fisher, Archbishop of Canterbury, declared the motion carried and then called the whole assembly to stand, as he led the members in prayer for the blessing of God on this new venture. The World Council of Churches was in being; page 719 of the *History of the Ecumenical Movement,* which records these events, bears as its caption the simple words "AT LAST."

It must not be supposed that this happy result had been reached without difficulty. Certain great churches, such as the

Church of Rome and that of Moscow, for different reasons had refused to have anything to do with the new Council. Some of the great free church bodies, notably those with a Baptist or Congregational tradition, were deeply anxious lest the Council should from the start try to transform itself into a superchurch, regardless of its declarations in favor of the freedom and autonomy of every individual church. Some conservative sections of the churches had convinced themselves that the Council was a dangerous spearhead of extreme liberalism and backed up by a good deal of ill-applied American money carried on a vicious campaign of falsehood and misrepresentation. But on the whole the Christian world, and even the world outside the churches, seemed to feel that a great event had taken place. "Why didn't they do it long ago?" was a comment not infrequently heard from laymen in those days.

Then the World Council had to settle its own constitution. The basis had already been formulated. The World Council had taken over the formula that had served Faith and Order so well and had declared itself to be "a fellowship of Churches which accept our Lord Jesus Christ as God and Saviour." It was well known that not all churches were entirely satisfied with this basis; some would have liked it to say more, and others would have liked it to say less. Behind the very innocuous resolution concerning possible changes in the basis, to be found on page 115 of the official report, lies a curious little piece of unrecorded history.

Under pressure from some churches which desired revision, the committee which dealt with such matters was in process of accepting a resolution which could have been interpreted as meaning that the basis had been only provisionally accepted, and was liable to be extensively revised. At this moment a member of the World Council staff, who had been too busy to attend earlier meetings of the committee, came in, was horrified to discover what was happening, and made a strong speech against any change in the basis being made or considered. Some conservative churches had joined the Council only with considerable hesitation. Any suggestion that the affirmation of faith in Jesus Christ as "God and Saviour" might be weakened would cause them seriously to reconsider their membership in the

Council. The passionate support given to this unexpected intervention was such that the original resolution was entirely dropped, and instead the Central Committee, though permitted to receive suggestions from the churches regarding possible change, was ordered "to keep its study of possible changes within the Christological principle set forth in the present basis."

Sections met and sections reported—on the church and its divisions, on the problems of evangelism, on the church and the disorder of society, on the church and international disorder. These documents have become part of ecumenical history, and can be found in the appropriate places. Each has formed the starting point for further ecumenical study and activity. That which aroused the greatest interest at the time and the sharpest criticism from both sides of the great political division in the world was the report on the church and the disorder of society. It was, naturally, an unusual and piquant event to have on the same platform and at the same meeting John Foster Dulles, not then so famous as he afterwards became, but already well known as a stalwart defender of the Western understanding of freedom and economic order, and Joseph Hromadka, the Czech theologian, who according to his own oft-repeated declarations has never been a communist, but has gone further than most Christians to accept the Eastern revolution as an act of God in history and to support the kind of peace propaganda that the Western nations have not on the whole felt able to approve. In such a setting a gathering of archangels would hardly have been able to produce a formula acceptable to everybody. It is not surprising that in the next few weeks the World Council was attacked by Moscow as a lackey of American capitalism, and by financial circles in New York as a dangerous spearhead of communist-inspired activity in the West. It is just possible that it kept exactly to the middle line of Christian honesty and obedience.

Such an Assembly could hardly meet without sending out a message to the churches and to the world. Only those who have participated in the framing of such a message can have any idea of the difficulties involved in such work. Not a single word of the first draft of the message survived unaltered into its final form.

To start with, members of the special committee appointed

to frame the message were not in the least in agreement as to what needed to be said. Some, like the Bishop of Chichester, felt that what was needed was a rather sharp and pungent message to prick and sting the consciences of men. Others took the view that in a day of such widespread distress the message should have a more consoling character: "What men need to know," said one famous German theologian, "is that there is a Good Shepherd, and that he is available to them." A layman of immense international experience remarked that the only effective message that can ever be sent either to church or world is, "Believe in the Lord Jesus Christ and thou shalt be saved." Three members of one subcommittee, appointed to work on the message, happened to have been missionaries in South India; they spent part of their time translating their draft rapidly into Tamil to see whether it would "go" in a non-European idiom. This draft fared little better than any other of the early efforts. Discussion and revision went on until almost the last moment before the presentation of the Message to the Assembly in plenary session.

As is so often the case when a document is the product of many hands and many minds, the message of the First Assembly of the World Council of Churches is marked neither by eloquence nor by profundity of thought. But it does contain certain phrases which have graven themselves deeply on the minds of all who care for the unity and renewal of the church of Christ:

> Christ has made us His own, and He is not divided. In seeking Him we find one another. Here at Amsterdam we have committed ourselves afresh to Him, and have covenanted with one another in constituting this World Council of Churches. We intend to stay together. We call upon Christian congregations everywhere to endorse and fulfil this covenant in their relations with one another. In thankfulness to God we commit the future to Him.[2]

"We intend to stay together." This was the operative word. And over twelve years the churches have lived up to their good resolutions. One or two small churches have withdrawn from the

[2] *The First Assembly of the World Council of Churches,* p. 9.

Council for reasons that seemed good to themselves. but their loss has been more than offset by the faithfulness of the great majority and by certain gains that will come before us in another chapter.

But what did it all amount to, and why have so many Christians, deeply versed in the affairs and in the history of the church, come to regard Amsterdam 1948 as one of the great watersheds of history? What distinguished this meeting from all that had gone before was that here, for the first time, we encounter the solemn act of the churches as churches.

We have noted from time to time the growing engagement of the churches as such in ecumenical endeavor. At this point it will be appropriate to draw attention once more to the revolution that this involved. In the nineteenth century work for closer fellowship among Christians had been undertaken almost exclusively by voluntary societies—either such international Christian groups as the Young Men's Christian Association and the World's Student Christian Federation or the missionary and Bible societies, which found themselves driven by the circumstances of their work into closer co-operation than that practiced by other Christians. To such efforts in favor of Christian fellowship the churches took up attitudes which varied between qualified favor and suspicious disapproval. Edinburgh 1910 marks the climax of that period and faintly indicates the beginning of another. Those who met at Edinburgh came almost exclusively as the representatives of missionary societies, some of which had little if any connection with the organized churches of Christendom. None of them had come as the official representative of a church; the churches as such were entirely uncommitted by anything that was said and done at Edinburgh.

Already at Stockholm 1925 we note a change. Quite a large proportion of the delegates came on behalf of and appointed by their respective churches. And this was increasingly true of all the succeeding conferences to which we have had occasion to make reference. It was always the desire of the ecumenical pioneers that the churches should come to take responsibility out of the hands of the volunteers who had first found the way. Until 1948, however, ecumenical activity found itself marked by the service is one of the clearest signs that "ecumenism" has rea arrived. This is something that even the busiest churchmen mu take seriously, something to which they may be proud to devc some part of their already overcrowded lives.

How does the World Council work, and what does it do?

The events that catch the headlines are the great Assemblies, t one of which we shall come later in this chapter. But perhap these are really the least important of the doings of the Worl Council and its allied bodies.

All the time it is carrying on an enormous task of service tc refugees and other unhappy and homeless people. Some Russian "Old Believers," having fled from the revolution in 1917 and lived for many years in China, were later found living in great distress in the Philippines and in Hong Kong, after a second flight from communism. It seemed that new homes might be found for them in Brazil and Paraguay. Naturally, the World Council had on the spot in South America a British citizen of Russian origin, who spoke Russian as his native language. These things do not ordinarily get into the papers; they are part of the lifeblood of ecumenical activity.

Perhaps more important than the great meetings are the small gatherings, where business can be carried on in a more direct and intimate fashion. Here a vital part is played by the Ecumenical Institute at Bossey near Geneva. It is strange that Bossey is doing little of that which it was brought into being to do, and yet how indispensable it has become in the life of the churches. Originally, Rockefeller gave the money first to rent and then to buy this beautiful country house, in quiet surroundings about fifteen miles from Geneva, in order to serve as a lay training center. Young people were to come from various countries, to be inspired with new visions, and to go back to take the lead among the young people of their own churches. Just after the war, half of Europe was unemployed, and it was possible to bring young people together in this way. As early as 1947 it was clear that the original plans were quite unpractical. Now Bossey offers for the four winter months a period of study for theological students, and a shorter three-week course in the summer, also for theological students. All the time conferences are going on. Laymen do come to them, but the majority of those who take part are in

excitement or the discredit which attach to the activities of the enthusiast, the amateur, the prophet, or the adventurer. But now all this was at an end.

The World Council is, as its name suggests, genuinely a council of churches. Its members are not individuals or groups or societies or special interests. They are churches, independent responsible bodies, which have decided in favor of membership, and have been formally accepted by the responsible bodies of the Council. This statement must be taken in its exact sense. The Council is not a synod; it cannot enact canons or decrees which will be binding on any church. Its recommendations or decisions will carry just that weight which they derive from the guidance of the Holy Spirit at that particular moment and no more. But when the Assembly at Amsterdam declared that "we intend to stay together," this was not the utterance of a group of Christian individuals, swayed by the emotions called out by fellowship in a great assembly. It was the carefully considered affirmation of a group of men and women, who knew themselves to speak as the chosen and accredited representatives of the churches. The churches have stood by what they there said. It is the churches that have resolved to stay together in this new venture. And that is something new in the history of the churches of Christ.

XII

Evanston and Ecumenical Dangers

On the day after the ending of the Amsterdam Assembly of 1948 the whole spirit and character of the World Council of Churches changed. It could not be otherwise. During the long years "in process of formation," the World Council had been a pioneer body, working toward a still uncertain future. It had been under the direction of men who, while not irresponsible, were not responsible for the official expression of the views of any church and were in a very real sense of the word adventurers. Now what had been fluid had crystallised; indefinite lines had hardened into a very definite shape. Such things are inevitable, as tentative organization gives place to definition, and experiment becomes limited by precedent. But some of those who lived through the earlier and freer days have never quite reconciled themselves to the changes that have taken place.

In the new order of things it was clear that a far more important role would be played by official church leaders, and in particular by the great church bureaucrats, that special type more notably present in the American scene than elsewhere. It may seem invidious to select for notice one rather than another, but it may be well to take a brief glance, by way of illustration, at two of the men who have given yeoman service to the World Council movement in its second phase.

By universal consent Bromley Oxnam would be regarded as one of the outstanding leaders of the Methodist Churches in America. At the age of forty-five he was called to the episcopate of that church, serving first in Omaha and then in Boston. When the Amsterdam Assembly met, he was Bishop of the Methodist area of New York. From early days he has had a deep interest in social affairs. It is significant that one of his earliest books (1923) bears the title *Social Principles of Jesus.* Several among

his later books have followed up this early interest. This has l
quite enough to get Bishop Oxnam into trouble with those
believe that any interest in such problems is a sure sign of
cipient communism or worse. During the lamentable perioc
the dominance of Senator McCarthy, Bishop Oxnam had to
dure a series of wanton and cruel attacks, which shocked
disgusted his friends throughout the ecumenical world.
through it all he has carried on as a man who, while shoulder
an enormous load of administrative work, has never forgot
that the first business of the church is to preach the gospel
Jesus Christ.

Franklin Clark Fry, surprisingly, has not yet reached the
of sixty. At the age of forty-four he was called to the exal
position of president of the United Lutheran Church of Ameri
and has been reelected for period after period of service. As
modestly explains, half of the electors thought that they w
voting for his grandfather, the other half that they were voti
for his father, and so at that early age he was chosen for a po
tion that is usually reserved for patriarchs. Fry is not a writer.
the world he is best known as an administrator and as a force
but fair-minded chairman. At Amsterdam he was chosen as vi
chairman of the Central Committee of the World Council
Churches, and later succeeded Bell as chairman. It was thoug
wise from the start to have the Lutheran churches of the wor
closely associated with the high command of the ecumenic
movement. A better choice could not have been made. Fry, wi
an apparently unlimited capacity for this kind of work, is al
treasurer of the Lutheran World Federation and president
Lutheran World Relief. But no one who knows him has any doul
as to when he is happiest. One of the delegates to the I.M.
Assembly in Ghana in 1958, idly turning on the radio on Su
day morning, heard an American voice plainly and forcibly se
ting forth the gospel of Christ. He wondered who the speake
could be; at the end of the address the announcer said, "Yo
have been listening to Dr. Franklin Clark Fry."

To be a member of the Central and Executive Committees o
the World Council is not a sinecure. That men who are alread
carrying so heavy a load in their own churches and in America
affairs should be prepared to give up so much time to ecumenica

some way professional Christians. Yet this too is an invaluable part of ecumenical life. The first director was Hendrik Kraemer, who brought to it his vast experience and his alert and questing mind, ever moving out in fresh directions. It is always difficult to get good lecturers for the theological students' courses—distinguished men and women are tied by their own work. But what matters far more is the education that the students are giving one another, in sessions that are often prolonged into the early hours of the morning, or in quiet evening visits to the village and the opportunities of entertainment that it offers. It is hard to say exactly how students are changed by these experiences; it is safe to say that those who pass through them unchanged are very few.

Necessarily, however, a good part of the life of the movement is expressed in its formal committees, meeting regularly every year. A large part of the business is so dull that any record of it must also be dull. But every year matters come up that are of more than passing significance. We may take as an example the meeting of the Central Committee held in Toronto in 1950. Here several matters of more than ordinary moment had to be dealt with.

The North Koreans had invaded South Korea. For years everyone who knew anything of the Far East had seen this coming. The Americans had left the South Koreans with a police force; the Russians had provided the North Koreans with airplanes, tanks, and heavy artillery. As early as 1948 Korean Christians had been saying to their friends, "Don't you realise that this is the front line? This is where it is going to start." So Christian opinion was perhaps less startled by the invasion than world opinion as a whole. Nevertheless, it was clear that a situation of the utmost gravity had arisen. President Truman had ordered American troops into Korea; the United Nations had approved a "police action" for the restoration of order and peace. Should the World Council of Churches say anything at such a time or not? In 1946, together with the I.M.C., it had brought into being the Churches' Commission on International Affairs to educate the Christian conscience on precisely such problems as this. It seemed to many that the time had come to speak out.

After long and sometimes heated discussion the Central Committee accepted a statement "on the Korean Situation and World Order." This statement lacked nothing in clarity and went very far in supporting the Western interpretation of the situation:

An act of aggression has been committed. . . . Armed attack as an instrument of national policy is wrong. We therefore commend the United Nations, an instrument of world order, for its prompt decision to meet this aggression and for authorizing a police measure which every member nation should support. At the same time, governments must press individually and through the United Nations for a just settlement by negotiation and conciliation.[1]

It is easy to pass such resolutions in the quiet seclusion of a Christian meeting; it is not always possible to foresee what the consequences of such action will be. We do not know what may have been in the minds of the North Korean leaders when they launched the invasion. We do know that the thousands of young Chinese who launched themselves recklessly on the American machineguns regarded themselves to a man as martyrs in the Asian cause, as willing victims of unscrupulous aggression carried out by the Americans, heirs of the colonial wickedness of the European peoples, against Asian freedom. The Statement confirmed the Church of Moscow in its belief that the World Council is a lackey of American capitalism. For years it made more difficult the rapprochement between Chinese Christians and their friends in the West. And yet perhaps it was right for the World Council to speak out; it is very hard to know exactly when it is right to speak the truth and shame the devil.

Then the Central Committee had to say something about the nature of the World Council, what it is and what it is not, in relation to the churches. Dietrich Bonhoeffer had put the question neatly in a German phrase that simply cannot be translated into English—*Ist die Oekumene Kirche?* What he meant was to ask whether the ecumenical movement is really *churchly,* in the sense that it springs from some deep apprehension of what the church in its inmost nature really is. Or is it just a matter of ecclesiasti-

[1] *Minutes and Reports of the Third Meeting of the Central Committee (Toronto, Canada,* July 15, 1950), p. 91.

cal carpentry, patching together disparate entities for purely pragmatic reasons?

The Committee had before it a document prepared by its general secretary. By the time discussion had ended, not much of the original document was left, but the statement on "the Church, the Churches, and the World Council of Churches" marks a real advance in ecumenical thinking. First of all it states a number of things that the World Council is not, and must never become. In particular "The World Council of Churches is not and must never become a Super-Church." Then it goes on to define eight assumptions on which the whole work of the movement is based. It would take too much space to cite these in full;[2] one specimen will serve to illustrate the mixture of theological and personal concern by which the movement lives:

(8) The member Churches enter into spiritual relationships through which they seek to learn from each other and to give help to each other in order that the Body of Christ may be built up and that the life of the Churches may be renewed.

Thirdly, an apparently trivial matter, the Committee had to decide where it would next meet. The text drily states that "the General Secretary reported that the Executive Committee . . . had canvassed thoroughly the possibility of a meeting in Asia, but that financial reasons had made it appear impossible to hold the meeting there." Behind this lies something of real importance. From the beginning friends of the World Council have been troubled by its overwhelmingly Western character. Representatives of the younger churches are there and are listened to with respect, but, as they themselves say, they regard themselves as ambassadors for more than half the world, although the greater part of that world which they represent is not yet Christian. A member of the World Council's staff had pleaded passionately that the next meeting of the Central Committee should be held in Asia or Africa, and that thus a public declaration should be made of the World Council's recognition of its universal character. He was overruled. In 1951, Miss Sarah Chakko,

[2] The document is to be found in the *Minutes and Reports of the Third Meeting of the Central Committee,* pp. 84-90.

whose early death robbed the World Council of its first woman president, had better luck. She said bluntly, "If you don't meet in Asia before the next Assembly, you may as well put up the shutters and stop calling yourselves the World Council of Churches." In face of this Asian determination financial considerations seemed not to matter so much. In 1952 a successful and well-attended meeting of the Central Committee took place at Lucknow in India. The only contretemps was that many members, having learned from their geography books at school that India is a hot country, had failed to take seriously the warning that Lucknow can be a very cold place in the cold weather. The one medical member of the committee, Dr. Garcia of the Philippines, had his hands more than full of ecumenical work, caring for the members of the Committee who had succumbed to the cold!

Finally, the Toronto Committee had to determine the main lines of thought and preparation for the second Assembly of the World Council of Churches. In the preliminary discussions the idea of "the Christian Hope" as the main theme for the Assembly was brought forward by E. J. Bingle, formerly a missionary in South India, and at the time editor of the *International Review of Missions*. On the basis of this suggestion a paragraph was drawn up by a member of the World Council's staff and was accepted almost unaltered by the Central Committee:

The time has come when the World Council of Churches should make a serious attempt to declare, in relation to the modern world, the faith and hope which are affirmed in its own basis and by which the Churches live. . . . We think therefore that the main theme of the Assembly should be along the lines of the affirmation that *Jesus Christ as Lord is the only hope of both the Church and the world.*[3]

The intention of the Committee was quite clear. The aim was to produce a statement, in simple language, that could be read with understanding by the ordinary man. In a world that is so full of despair, why do Christians go on hoping? What is the basis of their hope? What has Jesus Christ to do with it all? Have

[3] *Ibid.*, p. 23.

the churches really any word of comfort for troubled humanity, other than the shallow optimisms which have been sheltered again and again by the tragedy of human happenings? The preparation of this statement was to be entrusted to a carefully chosen body of twenty-five. The plan of the Committee was to include a number of eminent laymen—T. S. Eliot and C. S. Lewis were particularly mentioned—who, while not professional theologians, have a proved capacity for helping the ordinary man to understand what the great problems of theology are all about.

Alas, never did carefully laid plans go so sadly awry. The eminent laymen did not appear. The Committee of Twenty-five was made up almost exclusively of professors of theology. From the very first day the discussion soared aloft into the most difficult realms of theology and never came down from them again. We have had a hint of such possibilities in the suppressed conflict at Stockholm 1925, between what the continentals regarded as the absurd optimism of the Americans and what the Americans regarded as the unbiblical pessimism of the continentals. Now this conflict was to come out into the open and to range through all the meetings of the Committee of Twenty-Five.

We can well imagine the confusion. The leading part was played by theologians of German speech, none of whom had a deep knowledge of English. The British and Americans were rather better equipped in the matter of language, but many of them found it difficult to follow the technicalities of language that German theology had developed in the years of separation from the thought of the rest of the world. Accurate translation of these technicalities is extremely difficult. It seemed that no meeting of minds was possible. The Germans felt that the Americans, having never really experienced the tragedy of the war and all its consequences, were still building sand castles, unaware of the raging tides of the world's great seas. The Americans felt that the Germans would not allow us any hope this side of the second coming of Christ, and that this pessimism would cut the nerve of the vigorous witness and service to which Christians are called in this day of opportunity. The controversy overflowed from the council room and provoked a storm of pamphlets and articles all over the world. It was strange that no one seemed to note the crucial fact that the word "hope" does not occur once in any of the four Gospels. With all this controversy behind and around them, it is perhaps surprising that the Committee of Twenty-five ever produced a document at all. But under the wise and patient leadership of Bishop Lesslie Newbigin they did produce something at last. It was not what the Central Committee had hoped for. The statement on "Christ the hope of the world" is expressed in such language that many of the delegates to the second Assembly at Evanston had no idea at all of what it was talking about. Instead of being a clear statement to church and world of that faith and hope by which the churches live, it was another of those theological manifestoes that leave the layman out of breath and gasping.

To the second Assembly we must now turn. It was almost inevitable, with American influence so strong in the Council (an influence which, to their eternal honor, the American members have never overpressed) that the second Assembly should be held in the United States. The generous hospitality of Northwestern University made it possible to fix on Evanston, a suburb of Chicago, as the site. So there from August 15-31, 1954 the multitude of delegates and visitors made their way. What happened?

As a spectacle and a demonstration there is no doubt that Evanston 1954 was an enormous success. It was front-page news in almost every newspaper in the civilized world. Visitors were innumerable. Literally millions of Americans began to understand for the first time what it is all about and appreciated that the ecumenical movement is a living force, to which they are linked by membership in their own churches. At the first Assembly everything had been experimental. Now the World Council was an established organization, meeting with confidence to carry out its own business—under the arc lights, indeed, of world publicity, but with a certain sense of intimacy and well-tried friendship at its heart.

But how far did it go beyond Amsterdam, in the clarity and challenging character of its utterances and its mobilisation of the Christian forces to their world tasks in the present day? The events are still too recent for a final judgment to be passed on them, but perhaps, when the time comes, history will say that Evanston 1954 did not actually say or do anything very original or epoch-making.

Its Message ends with some direct and pungent questions to the members of the Christian churches:

> Does your church speak and act against such injustice? . . . Does your congregation live for itself, or for the world around it and beyond it? Does its common life, and does the daily work of its members in the world, affirm the Lordship of Christ or deny it? . . . Do you forgive one another as Christ forgave you? Is your congregation a true family of God, where every man can find a home and know that God loves him without limit? [4]

Here no one can complain of obscurity; for once a great church body really was speaking in terms that everyone can understand and presenting a challenge which every single Christian must face.

A welcome emphasis in the reports is that on the laity—the Christian in his vocation. This had not been forgotten at Amsterdam. But here it comes out with new vigor and lucidity. Most Christians in the church are laymen; in the last resort the quality of the life of the church will depend on what they are and what they do. The World Council's department on the life and work of the laity is one of the most vigorous and fruitful branches on the ecumenical tree. It is strange that until Hendrik Kraemer published his Hulsean Lectures, *Towards a Theology of the Laity,* no single work of theology appears ever to have been addressed directly to this theme. If the department brings to success its current project of producing a book on the layman in history, it too will unquestionably have pioneered in a field which has been almost totally neglected by historians of the church.

Such are some of the positive gains of the Assembly, and others could be noted. But at the Assembly itself, and in the years that have passed since it dispersed, many friends of the movement have been more conscious of the dangers that surround the ecumenical movement than of the triumphs that have attended its growth.

There is first the plain fact that it is no longer new. In an

[4] The Second Assembly of the World Council of Churches, *The Evanston Report* (New York: Harper & Brothers Publishers, 1954), p. 3.

admirable phrase coined or popularized by Albert Outler, the ecumenical honeymoon is over. Now we know one another, and the first delight of discovery is over. We have said and done all the obvious things. What do we do next?

This has raised for many people the question of the frequency of assemblies. Naturally, the Student Christian Federation arranges a big conference once every four years—that is the length of a student generation. But was the World Council well advised when it planned to hold an Assembly every five years? It takes at least three years to plan such a meeting; if it has done any useful work, it takes more than three years for that work to be absorbed into the life of the churches. Big assemblies are very expensive and very exhausting. Six years were allowed to elapse between the first Assembly and the second. More than seven years will pass between the second and the third. But are these intervals not still too brief? Is there not a real danger that if the World Council meets so often, it will be betrayed into the fatal course of uttering platitudes and trivialities and will end by losing the regard of the serious part of mankind? Most of the great church bodies, such as the Lambeth Conference, find that one meeting every ten years is quite enough. Is this an example the World Council might be wise to follow?

The formation of the World Council presented a challenge to every church. It was not surprising that ecumenical action was followed by strong denominational reaction. In one sense this has been good. It was necessary for the churches to turn back on themselves and to ask in plain terms what they stood for, what they believed that they had to contribute to the common stock of the church's life. But in this course there may be certain hidden dangers. Every one of the large denominations now has some world-wide organization, of greater or less tenacity, and some kind of periodical world meeting. Even the Anglican Communion, which has suffered from an almost morbid fear of the setting-up of a second Vatican at Lambeth, has now appointed a whole-time central officer (the first appointment that of Bishop Stephen Bayne of Olympia) to watch over inter-Anglican relationships and the missionary strategy of the Anglican Communion. By far the best organized of all these denominational bodies is the Lutheran World Federation, with its head offices overtopping those of the World Council in Geneva. Whatever the World Council does, the Lutherans will do it too, and perhaps do it better. They have their service to refugees and their theological commission. They have gone beyond every other church in having a central committee for missionary work, a body that really does exercise an influence on the far-flung missions of the Lutheran churches. Is there not a danger that the churches, in this new preoccupation with their own world-wide affairs, may lose sight of the wider vision and may come to care less for the unity of all God's scattered people? This is not a necessary consequence, but it is a possibility that every friend of the ecumenical movement must take seriously today.

Of "evangelical" reactions to ecumenism we must speak in a later chapter. The World Council does well to take no notice of the scurrilous attacks of malevolent people. But one of the facts that must not be overlooked is that a large proportion of the "evangelical" churches, in the American sense of that term, is outside the ecumenical fellowship. There have been welcome signs of friendship, as in the careful study of ecumenical affairs recently made by one of the most notable leaders in the Pentecostal groups. But there is evident a tendency on the part of these evangelical groups to get together on a basis very different from that of the World Council.

The greatest dangers of all, however, lie in a very different direction. Ecumenism has grown up as a challenge. It looks as though it could be used as a convenient means for the evasion of challenges.

The greatest achievements in the field of actual union of the churches all took place before the first Assembly of the World Council of Churches in 1948. The World Council does not concern itself directly with church union, rightly regarding this as the field of the churches themselves. But there can be no doubt that to many people the formation of the World Council has come as an easing of conscience and a satisfaction to the craving for union: "This gives us all the union we need; why should we look for any other?" The World Council provides a place where men and women can meet to talk in freedom and charity, a place in which they can pray together, an instrument far better than any we have had in the past for common action and witness. Why spoil this paradise by seeking something beyond it? So men are inclined to talk. Is it just possible that we may become so occupied with the theory of union, with all the new problems of ecumenical relationships and the delicate diplomacy by which they are to be maintained, as to forget that the only way to unity is to unite, and that ultimately ecumenism must lead on to the hard and relentless duty of finding a way to unite organically with those from whom we are now separated?

Ecumenism and mission. How do these fit together? It seems that in the minds of many young people the one excludes the other. The one word is as popular as the other is unpopular. Given the title "ecumenical," they will undertake almost anything. The word "missionary" suggests the outworn pietism of the nineteenth century. "Ecumenical" seems to speak of large-hearted and genial tolerance, in which we try to understand one another, and to offer service without any strings attached. Awkward questions as to whether there is some radical difference between truth and falsehood may be left comfortably in cold storage. It must be recognized that there is much that is excellent in this point of view. One will meet young Americans all over the world, carrying out really difficult jobs with patience, cheerfulness, and a real desire to understand the point of view of others. But the ultimate questions cannot forever be evaded.

There is one word which is hardly ever found in ecumenical literature, the word "conversion." This is an unpopular word in many circles in America, perhaps because it is burdened by too many unhallowed memories. We need not fight for the word, but the idea is one that we cannot do without. The church exists only because in every generation people have been converted—from every kind of non-Christian faith or lack of faith and from service to the devil, the world, and the flesh. Unless they go on being converted, ecumenism will cease to be a matter of very much importance, since there will nowhere be any church to which it can be related. The general secretary of the World Council spoke prudently and exactly when he said that our major problem in this second period of ecumenical life is that the ecumenical movement must become more missionary and the missionary movement must become more ecumenical.

XIII

John XXIII and a Roman Council

WHO WILL BE THE NEXT POPE? THE QUESTION IS ALWAYS BEING asked, and the only true answer that can be given is that no one knows. There is an old saying at Rome that he who enters the conclave as Pope leaves it as cardinal—it is only rarely that the favored candidate is elected.

There are exceptions to this rule. Pius XII was elected at a time of grave disturbance in the world. He was known as a friend and pupil of his predecessor Pius XI; it seemed wise to continue in the known and trusted paths. But strange reversals of expectation do take place. The cardinals after all are human. Although on so solemn an occasion they put aside, as far as possible, their personal feelings and prejudices, they have their partialities and their dislikes, perhaps sometimes even their ambitions. Sometimes external pressures play a part, as when in 1903 the Emperor of Austria practically vetoed the election of Cardinal Rampolla. There is a tendency to choose someone rather unlike the preceding Pope, so as to have the advantage of variety. There is often a feeling that after the election everyone who was in will be out, and a great many people who were out will be in. This was certainly the case when Pius IX was replaced by Leo XIII in 1878.

In 1958 the situation was peculiarly complicated. Pius XII had kept everything in his own hands and had not even named a Cardinal Secretary of State. As he grew older, he found it increasingly difficult to make decisions; though it was customary for Popes to name cardinals almost every year, he had done so only twice during his pontificate. Certainly his appointments, when made, had been generous, and for the first time he had given to the College of Cardinals a non-Italian majority. But at the time of his death there were many gaps in the College, and some of those who had been regarded as most likely candidates for the papacy, notably Mgr. Montini, the Archbishop of Milan, were not even cardinals. Technically, the elected candidate need not be a cardinal; indeed, under Roman Canon law any male Roman Catholic over the age of thirty years can be chosen, but as a matter of practice for centuries the cardinals have chosen one of their own number.

So speculation in Rome and in the world was particularly vigorous in 1958. Some had thought it possible that a non-Italian might be chosen. It is, indeed, unfortunate that for 437 years no one but an Italian has been chosen as head of what rightly regards itself as the most international body in the world. But those most closely in the know thought it probable that an Italian would be chosen, that he would be old rather than young, and that he would be drawn from the ranks of the pastoral cardinals and not from among those who were exercising high administrative functions in Rome itself. This, if correct, would considerably limit the range of choice. Yet even among those who had made such calculations, few perhaps had given much attention to the chances of Angelo Giuseppe Roncalli, the aged Patriarch of Venice. Just at this time the presiding bishop of the American Episcopal Church, Henry Knox Sherrill, was laying down his office under the rules of his church at the age of sixty-eight. It seemed hardly likely that the cardinals would thrust a man of seventy-six into the most exacting office in the world. It is clear that the choice was difficult and complex. Ten official ballots were held, and behind these lay endless discussions and proposals. But when at last the white smoke from the Vatican told the world that a new Pope had been chosen, it was the name of Cardinal Roncalli that was announced.

No sooner was this known than people began to realize how much there was to be said for the choice. For a long time the French church had felt that it was neglected or misunderstood by the Vatican. Recently the affair of the priest-workers had not been dealt with entirely to the satisfaction of that church. The French Cardinals were determined to have someone who would understand their situation and their needs. Cardinal Roncalli had served for a period after the war as Papal Nuncio in France. One of the great interests of the Roman Catholic Church in modern times has been closer relations with the ancient Orthodox churches of the East. Cardinal Roncalli had been for no less than nineteen years papal representative in Bulgaria and Turkey; he knew these regions well and had learned some of their languages. And so the chorus of eulogies went on.

But if anyone supposed that this old man would be nothing more than a genial figurehead, they were in for a series of shocks and surprises. It was at once clear that the new Pope was going to have his own way in a great many things. To start with, there was the choice of his name. There had already been a John XXIII, that incredible swashbuckler Baldassare Cossa, whose morals would have disgraced any respectable barnyard, and who more or less ruled from 1410 to 1415. By taking this name, Cardinal Roncalli put the historians to a good deal of perplexity, but made clear that he had set his seal to the Roman view that the other John XXIII had never really been Pope at all. It is hard to imagine a greater contrast than that between the present Pope and his predecessor. Pius XII had been to the finger tips a Roman aristocrat, with all the finesse that belongs to his race. John XXIII makes no secret of his modest origins in the Italian middle class; he possesses the rather different gift of shrewdness. From the first day of his reign he began to show himself friendly, sympathetic and vigorous, sweeping aside a good deal of meaningless protocol and manifesting the zeal of a true Christian pastor. Discussions had been going on for years as to whether the number of cardinals ought to be increased from the figure of seventy, at which it had stood since 1586. Within a few weeks of his accession John XXIII had increased the number to seventy-five, apparently after very little consultation with anyone else, and raised to the purple many men of eminence who had been kept waiting by the long hesitations of his predecessor.

Then in January 1959 the new Pope made history by telling a group of cardinals that he proposed to call an ecumenical council.

This was news indeed. No council of the Roman Catholic Church had met since 1870, when the Vatican Council was prorogued in haste, to the sound of the guns of the French and Germans, already locked in the deadly conflicts of the Franco-German war. The Council was only prorogued, not dissolved, and probably it was the intention of Pope Pius IX to convene it again, when the political skies were more propitious. But many had wondered whether this Council would not, as a matter of fact, be the last of the long series. The Vatican Council had been brought together for one main purpose—to declare the Pope under certain conditions infallible. This it had done. It had affirmed that when the Pope, in his capacity as Universal Pastor, gives *ex cathedra* teaching on either faith or morals, then his decisions are *irreformabiles,* above criticism or alteration, not by reason of the agreement of the Church, but of themselves and of their own authority. If this is so, what need to go to all the expense and complexity of a council? Can the Pope not simply give the faithful such directions as they need, on his own authority, after such consultation as he himself may think fit with the cardinals and other authorities of the church? Many had reckoned in this way. In a moment of time John XXIII had blown all their calculations sky-high.

It is time to look back and consider briefly the attitude of the Roman Catholic Church to the ecumenical movement. .

We have already seen how the delegation of Christians representing Faith and Order had been received by Pope Benedict XV—with a mixture of fatherly solicitude and of inflexible firmness on the point of co-operation. Shortly after the Lausanne Conference of 1927, Pope Pius XI, in an Encyclical Letter commonly known by its first words, *Mortalium Animos,* made perfectly clear the official attitude of the Roman Church and its head to all non-Roman Catholic attempts to promote the union of the Christian churches. There is one way to unity and one only, return to obedience to the See of Peter and acceptance of everything that it teaches. With any other form of effort it is impossible for the Roman Church or any of its members to have anything to do:

This being so, it is clear that the Apostolic See can by no means take part in these assemblies, nor is it in anyway lawful for Catholics to give to such enterprises their encouragement or support. If they did so, they would be giving countenance to a false Christianity quite alien to the one Church of Christ. Shall we commit the iniquity of suffering the truth, the truth revealed by

God, to be made a subject for compromise? These pan-Christians who strive for the union of the Churches would appear to pursue the noblest of ideals in promoting charity among all Christians. But how should charity tend to the detriment of faith? [1]

In making this declaration the Roman Church has rendered a real service to the ecumenical movement. The perpetual danger of such a movement is that it may sink down into the acceptance of a woolly-minded friendliness as its goal. The Roman Catholic Church reminds it that what matters is *the truth*. Charity and fellowship are needed, but they are needed as conditions for an effective search after truth. Attitudes may differ. Rome believes that it already has all the truth and need not seek it elsewhere. Protestants must look with caution on any approach to Rome, because they believe that Rome has grievously erred from the truth and needs to recover it. But the fundamental conviction should be the same on both sides.

From the attitude expressed in *Mortalium Animos* the Vatican has never really receded. Yet at one or two points there has seemed to be a certain softening of the decisions of Rome in practical matters.

The World Council of Churches has always desired to hold the doors wide open for contacts, official and unofficial, with the Church of Rome. This does not mean, as some enemies have tried to make out, that the World Council is in some way a crypto-papist organization. It simply means that the World Council recognizes the duty of developing whatever measure of fellowship is possible with all who in any way whatever call on the name of the Lord Jesus Christ. It was in accordance with this principle that the Provisional Committee of the World Council, at its last meeting before the Assembly of 1948, authorized the presidents and the general secretary to invite a small number of individual Roman Catholics to be present at the Assembly as unofficial advisers. The Vatican soon made it clear that no Roman Catholic would be permitted to be present at the Assembly with-

[1] See G. K. A. Bell, *Documents on Christian Unity, Second Series* (London: Oxford University Press, 1930), pp. 57, 58. The full text of *Mortalium Animos,* in English translation, is given on pp. 51-63 of this book. The official title of the Encyclical is "On Fostering True Religious Union."

out its own special permission; ere long it had become quite clear that in no case whatever would such special permission be given. A few Roman Catholics were present at the Assembly as journalists; some others were in Amsterdam at the time as visitors, but there was no official Roman Catholic participation of any kind in World Council affairs.

In the following year the Holy Office at Rome issued an instruction to Roman Catholic Bishops on the Ecumenical Movement. That such an instruction was felt to be necessary in itself shows the wide extent of the interest aroused in the Roman Catholic Church. The instructions on the whole are highly negative. The document starts with the plain declaration that "the Catholic Church takes no part in Ecumenical conferences or meetings." It is largely concerned with warnings that Roman Catholics who take part in meetings with non-Roman Christians may be tainted with "indifferentism." Yet Roman Catholics interested in ecumenism have on the whole read this formidable document in a very positive way, as opening doors that had hitherto been shut. In the first place, for the first time it officially recognizes the existence of the ecumenical movement. It recognizes that meetings between Roman and non-Roman Christians will take place, and though the rules it issues for the conduct of such meetings are strict, it does not absolutely prohibit their taking place. Above all it clearly states that

> although every sort of *communicatio in sacris* is to be avoided at all such conferences and meetings, it is not forbidden to open or close these gatherings with the common recitation of the Lord's Prayer or some other prayer approved by the Catholic Church.[2]

So much for the official attitude; this is what it is, and there is no likelihood at all that it will change in the near future. But the moment one turns to unofficial Roman Catholic approaches, one moves in a wholly different world. Here one is conscious of an ardent, almost passionate, desire for the union of all Christ's people that often puts to shame those on the Protestant side who

[2] The full text of this instruction is to be found, in English translation, in G. K. A. Bell, *Documents on Christian Unity, Fourth Series,* 1948-57 (London: Oxford University Press, 1958), pp. 22-27.

are loudest in their professions of ecumenical interest. We have become used to division, and can put up with it. To the best Roman Catholics it is never anything but a cause of agony that there are Christians with whom they cannot worship and enjoy the fulness of unity. They believe themselves to know how unity can be secured. Yet they are clearly moved by the deepest charity towards those whom they now delight to call "our separated brethren"; perhaps as the years have passed, the accent has moved from the word "separated" to the word "brethren."

Attention may be called to some of the forms of fellowship which do actually exist between the Roman Catholic and the non-Roman world.

Roman Catholic students are quite extraordinarily well-informed about everything that happens in the ecumenical field. It is a common saying that if you want to know what is happening in this field, you should go, not to the headquarters of the movement in Geneva, but to Rome—there they will have everything at their finger tips! It is the remarkable fact that the three books which will perhaps rank as the most important ecumenical publications of the last few years are all by Roman Catholics—*Histoire Doctrinale du Mouvement Oecumenique* (A Doctrinal History of the Ecumenical Movement) by the Belgian scholar Canon G. Thils (1955); Fr. Maurice Villain's *Introduction a l'Oecumenisme* (1958) and the work of the American Jesuit Edward Duff, *The Social Teaching of the World Council of Churches* (1956).

More important than anything else is the movement of prayer. A Frenchman, the Abbe Paul Couturier of the Archdiocese of Lyons, was led to promote a movement for prayer that "our Lord would grant to His Church on earth that peace and unity which were in His mind and purpose when, on the eve of His Passion, He prayed that all might be one." Clearly this was something in which Christians, of whatever confession, could conscientiously join. The dates selected for the "Octave" of prayer were the week between January 18 and 25. This has been officially accepted by the World Council's Commission on Faith and Order, and each year notice of the Week of Prayer and suggestions for its use are sent out from the headquarters in Geneva. The death of the Abbe Couturier on March 24, 1953 caused no halt in the spread of a movement which was already firmly launched on the whole Christian world.

Roman Catholic scholars have frequently lectured at the Ecumenical Institute near Geneva; they have spoken with frankness and charity of the position of their Church, and their contribution has been warmly welcomed by successive generations of students. Visits in the other direction are less frequent, but they do occur. Not long ago an Anglican bishop, who has the unusual advantage of being able to speak something like intelligible French, spent a week in Belgium, lecturing in improbable places such as Jesuit Colleges, meeting students, talking with leaders in various groups interested in ecumenical things. He came away almost overwhelmed by the generosity and candor of his reception and with the warmest invitations to come again.

Both before and after his accession John XXIII had shown himself deeply interested in questions of union, especially with the Orthodox churches of the East, which he knows so well. It is against this background of official firmness and personal charity that his plan to call a council is to be understood. Over the past year nothing has been more widely discussed in the Christian world; it is possible that the Pope himself did not realise all the difficulties that would lie in the way of the fulfilment of his purpose.

He had declared that this would be an ecumenical council. But what is an ecumenical council? This is a word that has been used in many different ways, particularly in this connection. The Church of England recognizes as fully ecumenical (worldwide) only the first four councils of the series, up to Chalcedon in 451. After that the ancient churches of the Far East broke away. The divisions have never been healed, and the church has never again been one as it was before this separation took place. The Orthodox churches recognize seven councils as ecumenical; these took place before the great separation between East and West, in which the year 1054 marks one crucial stage. But the Roman Catholic Church accepts as ecumenical a great many later councils, such as the Council of Trent in the sixteenth century and the Vatican Council in the nineteenth, though only the Roman part of the Western church was represented at them, and though no other part of the church has accepted their decisions. Clearly we are not agreed in our understanding of the word "ecumenical."

Then there is the question as to who can call such a council. The first great Council, that of Nicaea in 325, was convened by the Emperor Constantine. The special responsibility of Christian princes in relation to councils is recognized, for instance, in the 39 Articles of the Church of England (Article XXI). In 1438 the Eastern Orthodox came to the Council of Florence, at which for a short time they were united with the Roman Catholic Church, but they came only because they were accompanied by *the* Christian prince, the Byzantine Emperor, whose presence alone would make the Council ecumenical—you can still see him riding his horse in Benozzo Gozzoli's splendid fresco in the Chapel of the Medici in Florence. But now there are no more Christian princes in the old sense. The Roman Church takes it for granted that the Bishop of Rome can convene a council at will, and that it is his authority and nothing else that makes it ecumenical. In the Eastern churches decisions of councils do not possess authority until they have been accepted by the whole church. In the Roman Church they have full authority from the moment at which they have been accepted by the Pope, and none at all until that moment.

Next comes the question of possible invitations to members of non-Roman Catholic churches to be present at a Council. If such an invitation were given, on what terms would these other representatives be invited to come? If they were to come merely as observers, without power to speak or in any way to influence the course of the discussions, it is hardly likely that any would trouble to come. But if they were invited to participate as well as to listen, a revolution in church history would have taken place.

Supposing that all intermediate difficulties had been overcome and that members of the non-Roman churches agreed to be present at a Roman council, what would they talk about? One often has the impression that Roman Catholic friends are hardly aware of the chasm in matters of faith that separates them from those with whom they long to be united, and of the way in which that chasm has deepened in recent years. It is paradoxical that Pius XII, the Pope who spoke in most earnestly affectionate terms of his desire for the unity of all Christians in one visible fellowship, took the action which, more than any other in hundreds of years, has created an apparently impassable barrier between Roman and non-Roman Christians.

In November 1950 the Pope promulgated the doctrine of the corporal Assumption of the Blessed Virgin Mary. Since that date, according to Roman Catholic doctrine, everyone in the world has been required to believe, as an essential part of the Christian faith, that the Mother of Jesus was raised up in body and soul to that state of glory to which it is God's will ultimately to raise all those who have believed in his Son. Christian churches vary in the degree of reverence which they accord to the Mother of Jesus, but almost the whole of the non-Roman world agreed in condemning and repudiating this addition to the Christian faith. It is true that for centuries the Roman Church had held this doctrine in an unofficial way. But there is an immense difference between pious opinion, things which the faithful *may* believe if they find them edifying, and the declaration, as infallible truth and as an essential part of the Christian faith, of something that half the Christian world regards as historically uncertain and in any case unnecessary as a part of Christian faith.

The non-Roman Christian world has been driven back on its foundations. For the doctrine of the Assumption there is not the smallest trace of authority in the Holy Scriptures. There is not the smallest trace of it in early tradition. What, then, is the basis of our faith? The non-Roman churches ascribe varying degrees of authority to tradition; they are all agreed that ultimately tradition must be subject to Scripture, that it is in the word of God alone that we find all things that Christians must believe as the expression of their faith in Jesus Christ. Is the Roman Church prepared for a reopening of some of these fundamental questions? Out of countless utterances on this subject we may select some words of a young French scholar of Russian origin, Fr. Jean Meyendorff. He first puts the question whether this proposed Council will be not merely "ecumenical" but *true:*

In any case, the Orthodox will not find it possible to take part in the Council, if the agenda does not include the question of a review of that immense and fundamental evolution which has taken place in the life of the Catholic Church between the ninth and the twentieth centuries. For it is this evolution which constitutes the main obstacle to the reunion of Christians in one *true faith.* Alas! Rome seems hardly to be thinking of the possibility of such a review.[3]

What attitude, then, have the churches of the world taken up towards the Pope's proposed Council? The answer is that there can be no question of taking up an attitude, since at the time of writing there is nothing to which an attitude could be taken up. Everything is fluid, and since the Pope's first declaration of his intention there has been no official clarification of what has been intended. So bodies like the World Council of Churches, while expressing great interest in the project, have been very careful not to say what they might do in a number of circumstances, which may never arise and which at present cannot be more than a matter of conjecture. It seems likely that the Council will be a purely Roman Catholic affair, of great significance to the Roman world and of considerable interest to the rest of the Christian world, since the Roman world does after all constitute half of the Christian world. There for the moment we must leave the Council.

It may, however, be appropriate to end this chapter with a few lines from the first Encyclical of the present Pope. Like his predecessor he shows a most earnest solicitude for the unity of all Christian people and goes so far as to address a direct invitation to all Christians who are not now members of the Roman Catholic Church:

Let this marvellous spectacle of unity . . . touch and move your hearts, you who are separated from this apostolic See. Permit us, in our affectionate eagerness, to address you as brethren and as sons. Permit us to entertain the hope of a return which is so earnestly desired by our fatherly heart.

Take note, we pray you, that our affectionate appeal to the unity of the Church does not invite you to enter a strange dwelling, but to enter the house which is common to us all, the Father's house. Thus we address as brethren all those who are separated from us, in the words of St. Augustine: "Whether they will or

[3] Quoted in French in *Vers l'Unite Chretienne,* July-August 1959, p. 61, and translated by the author.

not, they are our brethren. They will cease to be our brethren only if they give up the use of the prayer, Our Father . . . Let us love the Lord our God and let us love His Church, God as our Father and the Church as our Mother. . . . So, very dear brethren, all with one single soul, hold fast to God as your Father and to the Church as your Mother." [4]

Christians who are not of the Roman allegiance may think that the Pope has gravely underestimated the difficulties that lie in the way of union. All can agree in appreciating the spirit that underlies these noble and moving words.

AUTHOR'S NOTE: Since this chapter was written, it has become increasingly clear that the Council will not meet before 1962 at the earliest, and that when it does meet it will be a purely Roman Catholic Council, occupied with the discussion of the domestic affairs of the Roman Catholic Church.

[4] The first Encyclical of Pope John XXIII; translation by the author.

XIV

What Next?

WE HAVE BROUGHT OUR CHRONICLE UP TO DATE. NOW WE MUST take a glance at the future, and our sober narrative must take on, for the moment, the more exciting colors of prophecy. What is likely to happen to the ecumenical movement in the next few years?

The first answer to this question must be clothed in anything but exciting colors. It deals with "integration," one of those strange pieces of jargon that the movement tends to cast up in its progress, partly no doubt because so many of its leaders have to think in one language and speak in another. As we have seen, the modern ecumenical movement began in the sphere of missionary responsibility; then the two main streams began to diverge, and World Council and International Missionary Council have endured a period of not altogether easy coexistence. Naturally, for many years past there has been a feeling that the two wings ought to be brought together again.

Various steps have been taken in this direction. Since 1939 the two bodies have had a joint committee. (Owing to wartime conditions, this did not actually meet till 1946.) Since Amsterdam 1948 each has existed officially "in association" with the other. As we saw, the two co-operated in creating in 1946 one of the most effective of ecumenical bodies, the Churches' Commission on International Affairs. But when it comes to the question of "integration," in such a form that there is only one great international ecumenical organization and not two, we begin to come up against a host of complex problems.

There is, first, a purely technical problem. From the beginning the International Missionary Council has been a council of councils. Its members are the councils or conferences of missionary societies in the sending countries, and the Christian councils in the various lands of the younger churches. Missionary societies are related in one way or another to churches, but they are not themselves churches. A body such as the National Christian Council of India includes representatives of churches, of missions, and of a variety of corporations such as the Bible societies, which are strictly speaking neither missions nor churches. The World Council, as its official name implies, is a council of churches. Only church bodies, which pass the Council's definition of what a church should be, a definition not entirely satisfactory to all churches, are eligible for membership. Certain other great international bodies such as the Y.M.C.A. and the Student Federation have a standing fraternal relationship to the World Council, but they cannot qualify for membership and can exercise no official influence on its policy. It is clear that any form of union between I.M.C. and W.C.C. is going to demand the exercise of a considerable amount of ingenuity.

The necessary ingenuity has been available. The Joint Committee of the two bodies has produced a plan which was felt to be workable and which secured a considerable measure of approval from members of the Central Committee of the World Council in 1957. Conveniently, the I.M.C. was holding an Assembly in Ghana in January 1958, and here "integration" was one of the main subjects for discussion. Some may have thought that, with the preparations so carefully made and with such obvious advantages in union, the matter would go through almost without discussion. If so they were to be severely disillusioned—in the ecumenical world things never go quite so easily as planners have hoped and expected!

The manner of presentation of the theme was, to say the least, unfortunate. The first three speakers were all Americans; all had been deeply engaged in the earlier planning, and all were strongly in favor of integration. It is not surprising that some delegates felt that this plan was being imposed upon them, without freedom to say "yes or "no." The immediate result of this introduction was that Max Warren rose and spoke to the subject for a full half hour. This was in itself important. The Rev. Canon M. A. C. Warren, general secretary of the Church Missionary Society in London, is recognized throughout the churches as one of the few first-rate thinkers on missionary problems in the whole Christian world. His monthly Newsletters, each one devoted to a careful survey of some area of the world or some field of special Christian concern, are masterly and contain some of the most up-to-date thinking on missionary affairs that is available anywhere. His speech was unusual. He started by saying that he was going to vote for integration, but that he would do so with a heavy heart because of the evils that he saw almost certainly following on the vote.

What were these evils? There was far more opposition to "integration" than had been foreseen. There was a feeling in some parts of the missionary world that the World Council and its leaders were not really interested in the preaching of the gospel in the world, and that if the I.M.C. were absorbed by the already larger body, the missionary interest would simply be lost. It would then be necessary to create a new I.M.C. to take the place of the body that had been killed by integration. Some felt that each organization was already, if anything, too large and that amalgamation could produce only a completely unmanageable monster. But by far the most serious opposition came from those who would call themselves "evangelicals" or "conservative evangelicals." We must distinguish sharply between this group and those responsible for the vitriolic and baseless attacks on the World Council and its leadership to which we have referred more than once.

To make clear the nature of this opposition, the best method will be to use a rather long quotation from a letter written more than eighteen months after the Ghana Assembly, temperate in tone and from the pen of a man who has friends in many camps:

The chief reason why the typical Conservative Evangelical is uninterested in the World Council of Churches is seldom theological . . . the typical Conservative Evangelical is seldom a good denominational man. He is normally more concerned with getting on with his work for Christ in the district in which he lives than with synods, assemblies and central committees. He is normally very willing to stretch a hand across denominational barriers at the local level, whenever he thinks there is a practical value in so doing. . . .

Then you seem to overlook that there are prominent elements

in the W.C.C., which do not really want to make the movement all-embracing. We have to face the fact that there are Liberals who regard the Conservative Evangelical with horror, especially if he belongs to a "fringe" sect. . . . It is not sufficient to write of the "neglect" of this side of Christianity; if it had been only this, it could be healed without too much difficulty. We are dealing with an active hostility on the part of a small but influential section of W.C.C. leadership. . . .

An interesting commentary on this is the way in which the International Missionary Council was able to build up a very much wider co-operation than the W.C.C. has achieved, at least among Protestants. The elements that are pressing most strongly for W.C.C.-I.M.C. integration are fully aware that it will lead to a breakdown in much of the missionary co-operation that now exists, but they seem to be indifferent to the fact so long as the bigger united body can be set up. It is doubtless unfair, but is it too unfair, if I suggest that the motto of many in the Ecumenical Movement would seem to be not "That they may all be one," but "That all the more respectable of them may be one"? [1]

It is always good to see ourselves as others see us. Not every word of this comment will be accepted as gospel by those who have long been concerned in the affairs of the ecumenical movement. It is, however, worthwhile to consider why this writer and others like him feel such deep concern at the direction in which things are moving.

A large part of Protestant missionary work is carried out by societies which look with suspicion on co-operation with others whose principles are not exactly the same as their own. In certain regions it has been possible to bring together such groups only on condition that they are not required to be related to the I.M.C., a far too miscellaneous body to meet with the approval of these cautious brethren. Thus, for instance, in Kenya in East Africa every single Protestant mission is associated with the Christian Council of Kenya, one of the best and most efficient of the councils set up in the lands of the younger churches. But this association is dependent on complete independence—at any suggestion that this Council should affiliate itself with any world body, a number of the associated missions would walk

[1] H. L. Ellison in *Frontier*, Summer, 1959, pp. 122-23.

out. One of the councils which just trembled on the verge of the I.M.C. was the Council of the Congo. As a result of the Ghana decision in favor of integration this Council has decided to withdraw from the I.M.C. In other regions of the world there are painful uncertainties and anxious searchings of hearts.

This may all seem rather remote and technical. But discussion of these issues is going to be very much in the air, until the next Assembly of the World Council of Churches is held in New Delhi in November 1961; it is possible that a number of readers of this book may find themselves called to contribute to official decisions on the matter. If so, there is one weighty consideration that must always be held in mind. We have as yet little clear guidance on the question from the younger churches most affected. The representation of the younger churches at the Ghana Assembly was regrettably small and inadequate as compared with Tambaram 1938. But those who were present expressed themselves, almost without exception, as enthusiastically in favor of integration. It seems that, in many regions, there is a real division of opinion on this matter between the missionaries and their friends in the local churches. Where missionary influence is still strong, it may be thrown against wider ecumenical union; where the younger church has a freer voice, the results may be different from those to be anticipated if too much weight is attached to mainly Western and mainly conservative utterances.

Hard is the path of ecumenical advance. It might seem that the Joint Committee of the two ecumenical bodies had quite enough to put up with in being sniped at so effectively by Warren, Birkeli, and other friends in the more conservative camp. But this was far from being the end of it. In quite another quarter a number of hornets were beginning to buzz audibly and angrily. For reasons that we have already explained, the Orthodox churches of the East dislike the word "missions" just as much as some leaders of the younger churches. In fact the Orthodox had never been represented at international missionary gatherings. But now a new thing had happened. The Metropolitan James of Melita, now Greek Archbishop in New York and a president of the World Council of Churches, but in 1958 special representative of the Ecumenical Patriarch of Constantinople in Geneva, was present at the Ghana Assembly of the I.M.C. The alert and watchful eye of this good friend of all the ecumenical leaders was on them all the time, as they hatched their plans for "integration." During the Assembly the Metropolitan James read out a statement expressing Orthodox views and anxieties about the proposed closer relations between the two large bodies. The Ecumenical Patriarchate, he affirmed.

> would never vote for any radical amendment of the W.C.C. Constitution nor would it be prepared to accept any change in the W.C.C. "ecclesiology" as declared in the well-known Toronto document. Finally the Ecumenical Patriarchate will insist on the two principles (a) that the sole aim of "missions" should be to reach peoples yet unconverted to Christ and never to proselytize among the members of Christian churches, and (b) that the "missions" should be "church missions" and should work for the up-building of the Church.[2]

A whole world of Christian history underlies these words.

While these pages were being written, the question of "integration" came up again at the meeting of the Central Committee of the World Council of Churches, held at Rhodes in August 1959. Naturally, Orthodox representation at the meeting was stronger than it has ever been before at such meetings, and a number of those present had not previously had any ecumenical education. It is not to be wondered at that once again anxiety was expressed at the idea of any closer association with those terrible and destructive bodies, "the missions." One Orthodox prelate urged the World Council to remain what it is—a Council of Churches. The Metropolitan Parthenios of Carthage, of the Greek Patriarchate of Alexandria, said frankly, "For us Orthodox, the word 'mission' is something which we fear. I don't know why. It's my tradition. For this reason, I say to you, 'Go slowly.' "[3]

In the two years that will elapse before the next Assembly of the World Council of Churches takes place, the International Missionary Council will have no very easy path to tread. It is

[2] *The Ghana Assembly of the International Missionary Council* ed. Orchard, (London: Edinburgh House Press, 1958), p. 163.

[3] *Ecumenical Press Service* (Geneva), August 28, 1959, p. 6.

perhaps providential that just at this moment it has been provided with a new leader, who can bring a fresh mind to bear on the many and complex problems that have to be faced.

The name of Lesslie Newbigin has come before us once or twice already. Before we end our story, we must take a closer look at one on whose wisdom and capacity for decision much will depend in this crisis of ecumenical development. The new general secretary of the I.M.C. has won distinction as scholar, thinker, writer, preacher, and administrator. If he had gone into politics or diplomacy or business, there is hardly any height to which his ambition might not have soared. Instead, resisting pressure on the part of his church, the Presbyterian Church of England, to remain in England, he accepted the vocation of a missionary in South India. Ten quiet years were spent in learning Tamil, reckoned by many the most difficult language in the world, in deepening his understanding of India and in the endless tasks of very ordinary missionary life. In 1947, at the age of thirty-eight, he was chosen as one of the first bishops of the new Church of South India. But at the World Council's Assembly at Amsterdam this slim, young bishop with the Presbyterian background was unknown by sight to the vast majority of the delegates. Ten years of authorship, of hard episcopal work, of endless ecumenical activity have made him one of the best known churchmen in the world. When Charles Ranson felt led to give up his post as general secretary of the I.M.C., there were many who felt that there was only one man in the world who could adequately replace him. The time and the man seem to have met.

It seems almost certain that in 1961 "integration" will become a reality. This may mean some withdrawals both from the World Council and from the I.M.C. It is hoped that they will be very few. Some will look with anxiety on a fusion that will create one immense organization for so many different forms of ecumenical work. But perhaps to those who have worked hardest and longest in the cause, the event, if it comes, will come as the crown and fulfillment of fifty years of endeavor. The modern ecumenical movement came into being in the heart of the missionary movement. Then for a time, by what has seemed to many an unnatural separation, different aspects of the movement fell apart. Their coming together again in one body may seem to be in line with the will of God, whose purpose it is to make all things one in Christ.

It is time to sum up the achievements of these fifty years and so to bring our story to an end.

It is only by a great effort of imagination that the churchman of today can realise what things were like in 1910. At that date there was not in existence one single organization through which regular international Christian consultation and action were possible. Not only so; many of the greatest and wisest leaders in the church thought that it was impossible that such organizations could be brought into being, and that if it were possible, it might not be desirable. Today a whole variety of organizations for thought, prayer, consultation, and action exist, and have come to be taken for granted as part of the permanent machinery of the Christian world. We can hardly imagine what it would be like to be without any of them.

In consequence there has been a steady growing together of the churches in friendship and mutual understanding. The differences are still extremely grave. No attempt to minimize them has been made in these pages. Yet it is just the fact that the leaders of Christian thought and action across the world are better acquainted with one another personally, are more closely linked together by subtle and mysterious bonds of Christian friendship than has ever been the case in earlier periods of the history of the church.

This moving together of the churches has expressed itself in this half century by the formation of at least thirty-eight united churches. Some of these have been large, some small. Many attempts to unite the churches have ended in failure; others are still being carried forward in hope tempered by anxiety. What is certain is that never before in the long centuries of the church's history has anything in the least like this happened. The nineteenth century was the great century of the church's expansion; so far the twentieth has been the great century of Christian union.

Even thirty years ago the word "ecumenism" was hardly known. "Ecumenical" was a headache to the journalists of the world and was constantly confounded with "economical." Now at least the word is familiar. It is not true that the ordinary church member has any clear idea of what it is all about; but at the time of Evanston 1954 any American churchman who read any church paper, or indeed read any kind of paper at all, knew that something was happening in the Christian world and that the churches were meeting in a way and on a scale that was without parallel in the previous history of the church.

All these are achievements of no mean magnitude. But what is yet to come is far more important than anything that has happened in the past.

It is still true that roughly half the people in the world have never even heard the name of Jesus Christ.

Does it matter? That question cannot be argued out in these pages; this is a study of ecumenism and not an apologetic tract. But as Archbishop William Temple once remarked with his usual shattering capacity for putting the most important truths in the simplest language, "If the Gospel is true for any man anywhere, it is true for all men everywhere." If the gospel is true at all, it is literally a matter of life and death for every man and woman now living in the world. When the general secretary of the World Council of Churches said that the missionary movement must become more ecumenical and the ecumenical movement must become more missionary, he was pointing to the consequences of a recognition of these elementary truths.

Churches have sometimes lived inward-looking lives. They have been concerned with the guidance and sanctification of their own members only. In that case they have not really been churches of Jesus Christ, the good Shepherd, who gave his life for the sheep. His church exists only as it is mission, only as it lives related to the ends of the world and the end of time, only as it is turned outward to men and women in all the needs and tragedies and darkness of their daily lives.

If the churches really began to live in this way, they would find that they could not do without one another. Take any area of the world you like; all the churches together are far less than adequate to deal with the social needs of that area, whether it be the juvenile delinquents of the East side of New York or the immigrants who are streaming all the time from Eastern Germany into Western. A great deal of the work of the church goes undone just because we do not know how to work together.

Every church should live all the time in awareness of its membership in the great fellowship of all those who today literally from China to Peru call on the name of our Lord Jesus Christ as God and Saviour, and at the same time in awareness of the unfinished task that lies before them. If all the churches were to work together to an intelligent and planned strategy and were to multiply five-fold their giving in money and in man power, they would still be unequal to the task of preaching the gospel of Jesus Christ to every creature.

To recognize these things means to live ecumenically in awareness of the greatness of the vocation of the church, in shame at the weakness and misery caused by our divisions, in readiness for a greater call from God than we have ever yet heard. And for each individual Christian awareness of these dimensions would mean a Christian life of an intensity and devotion such as usually lie beyond the horizons of our best imaginings. What this would involve has been so well expressed by Walter Freytag of Hamburg, another of the great missionary thinkers of the world, in his address to the Ghana Assembly of the International Missionary Council, that no words can better serve as a conclusion to this book:

> It is an illustration only of what I said, that those who live in the obedience of faith are part of God's action. An illustration only, not the matter itself. This fact, that every Christian is a part of God's action towards His goal, has a much deeper meaning. . . . The decisions of God's action are made in our life with Christ. There, more than the decision about our personal destiny takes place. There it happens that the Holy Temple of God is being built to its consummation. It happens or it does not happen, therefore according to how we live with Christ or do not live with Christ, we are a part of God's mission or we stand in its way. Therefore the Christian life cannot be lived without the wide horizon, the view of the world which God has in mind, the world which God loves. There God's mission is going on and it will be disclosed at the Day of our Lord.[4]

[4] *The Ghana Assembly*, p. 147. This wise and gentle man had played so great a part in ecumenical affairs that his sudden death between the writing and the printing of this chapter caused almost as great consternation in the Christian world as the equally sudden death of William Temple.

INDEX